HOW TO WIN THE WAR IN IRAQ

HOW TO WIN THE WAR IN IRAQ

Salvador A. Gonzalez

iUniverse, Inc.
New York Lincoln Shanghai

HOW TO WIN THE WAR IN IRAQ

iUniverse books may be ordered through booksellers or by contacting:

iUniverse
2021 Pine Lake Road, Suite 100
Lincoln, NE 68512
www.iuniverse.com
1-800-Authors (1-800-288-4677)

ISBN-13: 978-0-595-38110-4 (pbk)
ISBN-13: 978-0-595-82477-9 (ebk)
ISBN-10: 0-595-38110-3 (pbk)
ISBN-10: 0-595-82477-3 (ebk)

Printed in the United States of America

This book is dedicated to American and Iraqi military/civilian persons who have already and those who have yet to pay the ultimate sacrifice so Iraq can someday rejoice in Freedom, Religious Tolerance, & Democracy

God commanded, "*Thou Shall Not Kill*"
He gave no exceptions.

Contents

Introduction
MOST INVASIONS FAIL

Hasn't anyone learned that throughout the world's history no invading army has ever held on to its possessions? Some invading armies like the Mongolians, Romans and Greeks were able to rule and hold on to lands and territories conquered for decades and even centuries, but those possessions were eventually lost. Off hand, I do not know of any invading nation that has ever held on to possessions taken by force. It is arguable that in some cases the invader's demise came through the invasion of another state. Saddam's regime in Iraq is a perfect example of this. Would the United States have invaded Iraq in early March of 2003 if Iraq had not invaded Kuwait more than a decade earlier? Would Saddam Hussein still be in power today had he not invaded Kuwait? Did Saddam seal his own demise the moment Iraqi tanks traversed Kuwait's border in August of 1990? Did Adolph Hitler and Napoleon seal their own fates by invading the Soviet Union? Has America sealed its on fate by invading Iraq?

Before I continue I want to answer the last question above because it is extremely important. When the 19 hijackers slammed our own planes into the Twin Towers and the Pentagon, they had several purposes in mind: kill as many Americans as possible and plunge America into a war against the Muslim World. Anyone who dismisses the Taliban and Al Qaeda as a bunch of ignorant radical extremist bent on only killing Americans is absolutely right but they are missing the big picture and underestimating the enemy. As Osama Bin Laden planned his attacks, he must have known an attack of such magnitude upon the United States would precipitate a strike against Al-Qaeda and the Taliban in Afghanistan. 'An attack against a Muslim nation' Osama Bin Laden may have thought, 'will spark a global jihad against the U.S. and her allies.' Although the holy war anticipated by Osama Bin Laden may not have come to the fruition he desired, an American invasion of Iraq was just as good as it permeated the already incessant hatred against the United

1

States. How can America be certain that Osama Bin Laden had not strategically, with Saddam's help, moved all WMDs out of Iraq anticipating America's next move? How could the CIA, with an almost limitless budget and some of the most intelligent people in the country, have been so wrong about Iraq's WMD program? With all the evidence presented there are American people there are only 3 possible scenarios explaining what happened with Iraq's WMD's. 1. The weapons never existed; meaning the U.N. had been successful at destroying Iraq's WMDs. 2. The American people were deceived with old or fabricated evidence. 3. The weapons were moved prior to America's war mobilization.

With American troops bogged down in Iraq fighting a relentless insurgency we have left Iran and North Korea virtually unabated on their path to obtaining Nuclear weapons. As you will read later in this book, Iran does not need 100s of nukes to bring America to its knees. If what happened to the American economy after 9/11 is to serve as a gauge; then America must deduce the economic blow she will sustain if one atomic bomb is detonated in Times Square, Washington D.C. or any other major metropolitan area in the United States.

After 9/11, the mullahs of Afghanistan were quick to send their condolences to the American people. Osama Bin Laden on September 16, 2001 denied, on Al Jazeera television, any involvement in the attacks. Muslim and non-Muslim alike throughout the world believed him and refused to acknowledge irrefutable evidence of his involvement until about a year later tapes of Osama Bin Laden celebrating and admitting to the attacks were discovered and broadcasted throughout the world—even then millions of people still questioned the authenticity of the tapes.

Therefore, as mid-town Manhattan burns in the aftermath of a nuclear detonation Americans can rest assure that North Korea's Kim Young Il and Iran's Mullahs will send their condolences. Naturally, Iran will be America's first suspect followed by North Korea. Conceivably, both Iran's Mullahs and North Korea's Kim Young Il will deny any involvement in the attacks, as Osama Bin Laden denied involvement in the aftermath of the 9/11 attacks—just as many people believed Osama Bin Laden there will be many who will believe Iran's and North Korea's negations. Faced with such devastation America will be compelled to retaliate with massive thermonuclear strikes against Iran and North Korea; thereby terminating the existence of both those two nations.

The uproar after the annihilation of Iran will be exactly what Osama Bin Laden will have been concocting. (Think of the uproar a political cartoon has stirred-now image the annihilation of an entire Muslim nation) After such an attack upon the United States and a subsequent American retaliation Osama Bin Laden will have achieved at least one of two objectives: destruction of America's economic might and/or holy war by Muslims countries against the United States.

The scenario described within the next few paragraphs may not be too far fetched when we think of the animosity toward the United States by our so called Arab friends in the wake of Iran's destruction by the United States through nuclear means. Nation members of OPEC, at the violent demand of their citizens will cut off all oil imports to the United States; further destroying America's already dying economy in the wake of a nuclear attack. Someone with a quick mind will say, "If OPEC cuts off oil supply to the United States OPEC will lose a major buyer of petroleum." This may be true, but countries in Asia, with emerging economies and growing demand for oil, will be more than happy to buy the excess petroleum at discounted prices. Furthermore, it must be conceded that the leaders of OPEC, with the billions and billions of dollars (and maybe even trillions) in reserves, can easily weather any economic blow the stoppage of petroleum sales to the United States will bring. The United States with a meager supply of 45 days of petroleum reserves will be forced to ration gasoline at most extreme levels.

It is also possible that with a weakened United States countries of the Middle East will declare war against America and definitely against Israel. In America, due to shortages in Petroleum and a severely damaged economy, the people will need to adjust their living conditions to that of developing nations like Brazil and Argentina. And, just as economic woes caused the breakup of the Soviet Union, economic hardship in the United States may compel some states to secede from the union. And there you have it, the end of America, as we know it. (Let's consider this other factor; America is 8 trillion dollars in debt-wait add another million and another and another and another-catch my drift. With most of that debt owed to countries like China, will America be forced to capitulate some land in order to pay off the debt?) And centuries from

now the 19 hijackers will be reveled martyrs and people will speak of how a mighty nuclear superpower was decimated by men armed with only small blades. As absurd as this may sound, on the evening of September 10, 2001 it would have seemed ridiculous to think the twin towers would not exist by noon September 11, 2001.

Could a scenario, as the one described above be what Osama Bin Laden has been planning all along? Osama Bin Laden has said it himself, "Bush is easily manipulated". To me this means America's leaders are falling easily into Osama Bin Laden's plans.

Some of the most potent empires of the past have ceased to exist: Romans, Ottoman, Greeks etc, etc. Some who attempted to acquire empires have failed miserably. Japan suffered probably the most humiliating defeat of all. As the bombs fell on Hiroshima and Nagasaki, the once fierce and furious Japanese Empire was brought to its knees. After the second bomb dropped on Nagasaki Japanese citizens trembled in fear that their city would be next. The empire once feared by Asia had quivered and dissipated in a matter of days. Those who quietly gave up their possessions have remained but only as a shadow of their former self: Great Britain, Portugal and Spain. At the height of England's empire, it ruled most of the new world and had colonies throughout Asia and Africa. England is now mostly relegated to its group of islands.

With all these failed invasions how can America expect to hold on to a possession taken through aggression? America has engaged in wars for almost every generation since the signing of the Declaration of Independence over 230 years ago. In that time, America had not lost a war until 1975 when it withdrew in a humiliating defeat from Vietnam. Some will argue that the war in Vietnam did not start out as an invasion but rather an intervention. There is some merit to that argument but the fact remains that Americans, according to the Vietnamese, were invaders in a struggle between North and South Vietnam. Perhaps that is all it takes for a people to rise and fight; to feel invaded. It can also be argued that America's intervention in Granada and Panama were invasions and America won those conflicts. This is true but Granada was not an invasion and occupation and the island of Granada, with a population of less 100,000 citizens, is much too small to mount much retaliation against the United States. In Panama, the United States already had a strong presence and even so, America gave up its possession of the Panama Canal on December 31, 1999.

Although these two conflicts can be considered invasions they were not to the scale we have seen throughout world history. Other examples of invading armies losing are: Germany's invasion of Russia, England's invasion of the American Colonies, France invading Russia. In recent history and throughout history most invading powers have been successful at the outset but have failed miserably when trying to hold on after an invasion. History is littered with failed invasions and the death of great nations. Why should America be any different?

I want America to succeed after invading a country simply because I am an American by choice—in my personal opinion the best there is! I believe in America's ideals of freedom and democracy. I believe in capitalism—when it is properly checked. I believe in America's values of religious tolerance and freedom, justice for all and America's advocacy of inalienable human rights of every person on this planet. I do not see America as an invader; though it has invaded Iraq in the true sense of the word's definition. Nevertheless, I believe in America's noble intentions. I believe America does not wish to occupy Iraq any longer than it has to.

I believe America will exit Iraq when it has achieved its objectives of democracy and freedom for Iraq's people. Once this occurs there may never be a need for America to fight any other wars in the Middle East. The people of the region will see the Iraqi people prosper under a veil of freedom and democracy. They will see that America's intentions were always good and noble and they will demand freedom, social reform and will hold their government accountable of serving their needs and sharing the wealth that lies beneath their feet in the form of vast petroleum reserves. Small groups of individuals in countries of the Middle East have wealth unimaginable to any of us; yet, that wealth seldom trickles down to the people. Their people see America has a land of Satanists and infidels because that is what they have been taught to believe. Why is it that in Central America and other parts of the world, America is seen as a beacon of hope and freedom while in the Middle East America is demonized?

When I was a child growing up in El Salvador and overheard my grandmother talking about America I was profoundly curious. She talked about America as having clean streets and beautiful houses and no poverty. I can still hear my grandmother saying, "Dicen que alla no hay basura en las calles y la gente vive en casas bien bonitas y no hay pobresa." This translates to, "They say that over there, there is no garbage strewn in the streets and that everyone lives in beautiful houses and there is no poverty." Naturally, my young imaginative mind thought of beautiful homes, grand parks and clean evenly paved streets. I imagined a beautiful country where it was wonderful to play. At the time, my mother lived in America so I knew for sure she was wealthy as I often heard my grandma say that everyone in America was rich.

When my mother, after spending six years in America working in the sweatshops of Yonkers, Manhattan and the Bronx, arrived in the El Salvador and announced she was bringing my siblings and me to the United States I felt proud and privileged. With pride I announced to my friends, "I am going to America." I was looked upon with jealousy, envy and awe. How lucky I must have seemed to them. And so we migrated to the United States and though I didn't find the litter free streets, evenly paved roads and beautiful houses because we lived within America's ghettos, as an adult and a professional I have found the litter free streets, row upon row of beautiful houses and evenly paved roads. Even so, the poverty I experienced in America compares not to the poverty I experienced in El Salvador. The fact remains that never did I hear my grandmother refer to The United States as the land of the infidels and Satanists. Can you imagine how frightened I would have been after my mother's announcement? I would have probably hid behind the kitchen sink.

The people of the Middle East are taught from a young age that America is the enemy and that Americans are infidels. This vile and poisonous rhetoric is often times spewed from the pulpit. Karl Marx once wrote, "Religion is the opium of the people." Karl Marx was wrong on many many ideological principals but from his perspective he was right about religion because in his lifetime he had witnessed tyrannies exploit religion to repress their people. In the Middle East often times clerics use religion to repress their own people. While sex is oppressed, men like Uday and Qusay literally raped little girls. Furthermore, in Iran the use of poor uneducated little girls as prostitutes runs rampant.

The atrocities committed by Muslim extremist in the Middle East are unholy, callous and directed by Satan himself. Yet, they call America the land of infidels and Satanists. During the reign of terror by the Taliban in Afghanistan, hundreds of people were beheaded, maimed and put to death without trials for minor offenses such as seeming to oppose the Taliban. Men were beaten in the streets for not wearing their beard a certain length and women were stoned to death if caught in the presence of any man not directly related to them. I am not a scholar of the Muslim religion but I am quite confident the traditional Muslim teachings do not call for this type of barbaric treatment of another human being. Any act committed against God's law is inherently an act committed in favor of Satan.

Point people of the Middle East should consider

In the 1970, the United States, built the Alaskan pipeline. This pipeline stretches from Prudhoe Bay on Alaska's North Slope to Valdez. The pipeline traverses *through some of Alaska's most pristine landscape. All together, there are over 800 miles of pipes laid. Each Alaskan resident receives a stipend of up to $3000.00 U.S. dollars in royalties for the pipeline. How much does your government pay you for the entire petroleum pumped out of the land that is rightfully yours?*

Throughout the Arab world, the people are fed wrongful views of America. With no other outlets the people begin to believe what they hear, however ridiculous or absurd it may be. When listening to the rhetoric of Islamic extremist the people of the Middle East should keep in mind that in America beheadings, severing of limbs, stoning of women by government or religious groups are non-existent—though from time to time these type of barbaric acts are committed by demons those acts are always considered criminal! They must also remember that over 5 million Muslim live in America and with the exception of a brief period after 9/11, when some Muslims where harassed and threatened (In America we have a few extremist idiots as well) Muslims practice their religion in peace and safety.

With trillions of dollars in oil revenue going to Kuwait, Iran, Saudi Arabia and other Arabs countries since the discovery of petroleum in the Middle East in the 1940 it is conceivable many of those countries would have higher standard of living than nations of Europe and the United States. With such vast amounts of wealth, it is difficult to grasp how poverty can be so rampant. Poverty in Iran is so extreme and some people are so poor it is not even considered poverty but "miseria" (A word often used by my relatives in El Salvador to describe people who are live in card-board boxes or 'casa-de-carton'. As the reader you may be asking, "Why are they called "casas de carton". The answer is simplistic, the houses are made from card-board boxes.") Yet, through all their troubles why do they blame America? It is like blaming the sheep for being caught by the fox. They blame America because that is what is being fed to them by their own educational and government institutions. They do not stop to think that while Saddam Hussein built great palaces lined with gold the Iraqi people starved. Iranians do not stop to think that while millions of its citizens go hungry the Mullahs pursue a nuclear weapons program costing billions and billions of dollars.

I digress. The reason why you probably picked up this book is because the title caught your attention. This book, by no means, attempts to architect how to win the war in Iraq but rather it tries to provide the reader with some ideas as to how the war in Iraq can be won. I also wish to have my fellow Americans start asking our government for a clear road to victory and what it will looks like for us and the rest of the world when victory is finally proclaimed. Will we consider there to be victory when all American have pulled out of Iraq but Iraq is still in ruins, financially wrecked but Iraqi troops have replaced Americans soldiers in the fight against the insurgents? Will victory in Iraq be declared even though terrorists are still capable of attacking America and her allies? The central theme of this book is that America's leaders must galvanize the American people into winning the war. America must thrust its might into winning the war in Iraq! The consequences if we lose are grievous and perilous to our national security.

For the reasons you will read about later in this book, America cannot withdraw from Iraq. My heart goes out to Ms. Cindy Sheehan. She is advocating America's withdrawal from Iraq, but although her intentions are good, her premise is wrong. America cannot withdraw as it will cause foreseen and unforeseen calamities. However, it is imperative that Congress never allow an American President and itself to invade another country without what I will coin "**Irrefutable conclusive evidentiary confirmation of Imminent Danger to the United States**". America went to war on false and possibly fabricated information. As Americans we would never maliciously convict a person accused of a crime beyond a reasonable doubt. Therefore, America should not have invaded Iraq based on the information we had on WMDs; especially when thousands of both Iraqi and American lives were at stake. However, it is too late to argue the merits of invading Iraq so the point here is that Congress must never allow America to invade another country without irrefutable conclusive evidentiary confirmation of imminent danger to The United States.

The Iraq war cannot be won solely through military force. The old adage, "To the victor belong the spoils" is utterly true in this case. America has inherited a country devastated by a 10-year war against Iran, a war against the United States and its allies, 10 years of U.N. sanctions, Saddam's 25 years reign of terror and more war waged by the United States. The moment America took possession of Iraq by shear force America inherited all of Iraq's problems. America, is therefore morally and ethically obligated to rebuild the country. America cannot simply oust Saddam Hussein, train a couple of hundred thousand troops to guard the country and leave.

1

AMERICAN'S SUPPORT

Failure in Iraq is not an option

If the United States of America is to win the war in Iraq it must concentrate a significant portion of its military, industrial, technological and economical might into the rebuilding of Iraq's economy, infrastructure and police forces. This book aims to serve as a road map to winning the war in Iraq. The 5-prong strategy relies heavily on galvanizing the American people behind the reconstruction of Iraq at a level not seen since World War II when Americans stood behind their government by cohesively contributing to the defeat of the Germans in Europe and the Japanese in Asia. Europe was left decimated and almost bankrupt after the end of World War II. George C. Marshall however, came up with a 15 billion dollar reconstruction aid package for Europe. In my opinion, the Marshall Plan did more to stop communism than the 700 billion spent to fight in Vietnam and North Korea.

The Marshall Plan

The Marshall Plan implemented in Western Europe after the end of World War II, offered the European nations billions of dollars in reconstruction aid. Secretary of State George C. Marshall had enough foresight to realize that without the reconstruction of Europe, it would quickly fall for the false ideologies of communism. Communism is attractive to people in dire need because it offers the hope of a decent life by providing equally to all. Communism works great, until you throw in the human element. Then it gets real ugly as the poor stay poor and the rich get "ludicrously" rich—I have often said that Communism is equal to capitalism at its most gluttonous extreme. After World War II, most of Europe was ripe to fall victim to communist ideologies. The Marshall plan was so successful that by the early 1950's Europe was starting to stand on its own feet. But the Marshall plan did not only help Europe it also helped the American economy as most of the rebuilding materials were coming from the United States.

Without the support of the American people, the war in Iraq will be lost. Some polls indicate that support for the war in Iraq is at an all time low of about 40–45%. Few will not forget that at the outset of the war support was at 80–85%. If 3½ years after the war support for it has dropped by 40 percentage points where will it be in two more years. This is a frightening question because in 2 years more Americans will have died, Iran may have or may be very close to obtaining nuclear weapons and North Korea may have already tested an atom bomb. Furthermore, at the current rate of expenditure for the war in Iraq, (Approximately 1/2 Billion dollars per-day) and with the insurgency expected to continue for at least 2 more years it will have cost the United States almost ½ trillion dollars to maintain its presence in Iraq through 2007. By then America will be observing 4 years of continuous war with no end in sight.

Over half a trillion dollars is a large sum of money. This is a phenomenal amount of money for a country almost 8 trillion dollars in debt and an emerging tsunami or retirees.

Point to consider

An interesting note Americans must observe here is that insurgent type conflict has marred the Middle East for centuries—is America prepared to maintain a military presence in Iraq for several millennia? Saddam Hussein has been accused of using chemical weapons against his own people. That fact cannot be argued, but as horrific as his crime was, has anyone stopped to think why Saddam committed his crimes? Could he, as a ruthless dictator, with no regard for human life, with the exception of his own, have been attempting to put down insurgencies spawn by his rise to power? The answer to this question is probably a resounding, "Yes". I am not trying to defend Saddam Hussein as I think he is a piece of puke. What I am trying to say here is that Saddam may have been dealing with insurgents throughout his 25-year reign of terror in Iraq. Is America ready to keep a military presence in Iraq for 25 years?

How much is 8 trillion dollars

If 8 trillion dollars was equivalent to 8 thousand dollars Bill Gates would only have 43 bucks in his wallet.

Further compounding these monetary constrains is an out-of-control Health Care system with double digit inflation year after year. Americans cannot disregard an inevitable slowdown in the economy, which would further hinder tax revenue and thrust the United States into much more debt.

The Quick Thinker

Most of the debt is owed to Americans (Though this is quickly changing to debt owe to foreigners and sovereign nations). I totally agree and that is good but debt whether owed to a bank or other forms of lending institutions is still debt. Furthermore, this debt is not owed to the average American. This debt is owed to America's Multi-millionaires who, by the way, do not mind, lending money to a creditor who has never defaulted on an interest payment. If someone owed me 10,000 dollars but they paid me 100 dollars per month for the debt month after month and year after year (even after my original loan amount had been paid-off) I would not mind not ever getting completely paid. I would want the debt to stay out there for as long as possible. But that is outside the scope of this book.

How much is ½ billion dollars

The Board of Education for the city of Yonkers, New York plans to spend 402 million dollars for the upcoming 2005/2006-school calendar year. The U.S. will spend about that much in 1 day in Iraq.

500,000,000 Million dollars invested at 1% will yield you 5 million dollars per month.

Total private donations to the victims of hurricane Katrina has not come even close to exceeding what America spends in Iraq on a weekly basis.

Total donations to the countries ravaged by the Tsunamis have not exceeded what is spent in Iraq in only 2 days.

If Bill Gates, the richest man in the world, had alone, financed the war in Iraq, he would have gone broke during the first year of the war. By now he would have been seen at the corner of 34th and Broadway begging for loose change and a sign reading;

> *"Pleese Help*
> *Compooter lezons 4Food*
> *God Bless You."*

I can go on with these numbers forever and a day but the point here is that ½ billion dollars is a s#!t load of money.

Continue....

Without the support of the American voting public, creation of jobs and rebuilding of Iraq's infrastructure America's endeavor into Iraq is bound to fail as did the Vietnam War. Failure in this case would be disastrous for the United States and our allies as it will perpetuate a plethora of terrorist violence throughout the free world. Failure in Iraq will plunge Iraq into a bloody Civil War that will last for up to a decade and end with a dictatorship; bringing Iraq back to February 2003. If the United States cannot achieve peace, lasting prosperity and democracy in Iraq within the next 2–5 years then having spent a significant amount of dollars America will have two choices: walk away without victory or continue spending billions of its citizen's hard earned money fighting an undeterred and undefeated insurgency.

Point to consider

Some of the same military tactics used in Vietnam are being used today in Iraq. American troops must be given a lot of credit for their bravery in battle, but for a soldier on the battle field how much sense does it make to fight the same battle twice? In Vietnam American, soldiers would engage and defeat their enemies time after time. There was only one problem. American soldiers were fighting the enemy for the same territory repeatedly. The same scenario is being played out in Iraq. I do not think it takes a great military mind to realize that this type of fighting is plain stupid. A quick thinker will say, "Well, that's because you can't take over hostile territory and stay forever." This is outstanding thinking! Inherently, however, this is exactly where, in my non-military strategic way of thinking, invasions fail! Eventually the invading troops, from foot soldier to general, want to go home. And the people who live on the land return; only now more determined to defeat you because their homes and livelihoods have been destroyed by your invasion.

What I am trying to point out here is that throughout history, often times, victory has belonged to the General with new and creative ideas on how to wage war. Hitler swept through Europe with his Blitz Krieg tactic. The Gulf war was fought with precision guided missiles. World War I was fought with biological weapons and trench warfare. The United States cannot fight terrorism in a conventional fashion. In my opinion the United States committed a huge blunder when she invaded Iraq because she has left Iran and North Korea practically unabated in their pursuit of nuclear weapons as both nations know full well

American cannot fight them and Iraq simultaneously. Furthermore, with the pretext for invading Iraq now proven to be false, America's credibility on any intelligence will be perused and received with much skepticism.

Winning the war in Iraq is paramount to the future of the free world and to the United States. Losing the war will create new enemies throughout the Middle East and other parts of the world. Losing the war in Iraq will be reminiscent of the movie Independence Day starring Will Smith. Once it is discovered how to destroy the ships it is all over for the aliens. A defeat in Iraq will show America's enemies that patience and suicide bombings will cause America to cower and retreat. America is a powerful nation with great resources and might but those resources are not infinite and as full as its economic power is, it will not and cannot sustain the drain of fighting more than two or three wars year after year. While America spends millions and millions of dollars per day to fight the war in Iraq, the insurgents probably spend a few hundred thousand. A few hundred thousand may not be much when multi-billionaires back your cause. How much can it cost to brain-wash an 18 year old Iraqi to drive a couple hundred pounds of TNT into a building or American tank. It probably does not cost very much; in the meantime, that brainwashed 18-year-old damages an extremely expensive tank or vehicle. America cannot and will not be able to sustain such economic losses without hindering its own economic growth at home and forcing it to channel monies intended for its retirees and social programs to a stagnate war.

This book will not attempt to argue the merits of going to war in Iraq as it is a moot point and not worth discussing. The fact remains that the United States, almost 3 1/2 years into the war is stuck fighting an increasing insurgency that will only get worst as more Iraqi civilians die. Every time an Iraqi is killed, whether by the insurgents or Americans forces, the Iraqi insurgency gains in its ranks. On one side, the Iraqi's see the insurgents as an effect of what America has caused (an invasion). When an American kills an Iraqi, it adds more fuel to the insurgent's twisted form of logic. In their minds, the killing of an Iraqi by an American only demonstrates further proof that America is the enemy and must be ousted from Iraq. As Americans, we must try and place ourselves in the life of an Iraqi. Before Saddam Hussein's humiliating fall from power as an Iraqi you were fairly certain that if you kept dissenting political views to yourself and "hailed" the chief your life was not in any imminent danger. Under American occupation, what kept you alive for 25 years no longer shelters you from death or injury. Under American occupation, an Iraqi faces the threat of death or life altering injury simply by going to the market or stepping outside his/her home.

Some disturbing facts:

More Iraqi's die each day under American occupation than during Saddam's reign of terror.

Since America's invasion of Iraq in March of 2003 through July 2005, 25,000 Iraqi people have been killed. Iraq is a country of approximately 26 million people. If we apply the ratio of 25,000 people killed per every 26 million to the population of the United States it would mean that from March of 2003–July 2005 125,000 Americans would have died through violent conflict; suicide bombings, explosions, etc, etc. It is important to think of what affect that would have on the American people. Whom would Americans blame for those deaths? Would Americans blame the invaders or those fighting the invaders?

Therefore if you are an Iraqi citizen you are probably thinking, "Things were atrocious under Saddam Hussein but they are definitely worst under the Americans and their "puppet government." For Iraqi citizens, it is simple to blame the Americans for all your troubles. As Americans, we must look at the current economic, social and political deterioration from the point of view or an Iraqi citizen. It should follow logically that the Iraqi people will, regardless of who initiates an armed confrontation, blame Americans for Iraqi deaths. It is a vicious cycle that must be broken and the only way it will be fixed is by making absolutely sure the country prospers as quickly as possible. The questions before us are: How can we ensure the security of the Iraqi people? How can we rebuild the country when the insurgents constantly sabotage water, oil and even humanitarian relief efforts?

I am no military strategist or posses a great political mind. I graduated from Mount Saint Mary College, in Newburgh, N.Y. with a Bachelor's Degree in English and minor in Political Science. Throughout my life, I have enjoyed and studied American and world history. My only military experience was in the Junior Reserve Officer Training Corps (JROTC) of my high school and my only elected office held was in Middle School. Since graduating from college, I worked as a Life Insurance salesman and later in the IT industry.

I do, however, believe I have a clever mind and I like to think I have a little bit of talent for discovering new ways of tackling some complex problems. Given enough time I can solve almost any problem through the use of innovative strategies. A lot of what is written here may be erroneous and/or plain wrong, but the fact is that I don't see any one else providing us with clear and concise solutions to ending and winning the war in Iraq. All we hear from the right is more of the same; more war and training of Iraqi forces—reminds me of the beginning and end of the Vietnam War. Most people will recall that at the beginning of the Vietnam War American soldiers served as "Advisors" to the Vietnamese regime of President Diem. After a few years, it was obvious to America that the South Vietnamese either could not fight the North Vietnamese or simply refused to do so; and so American troops took on the responsibility of doing more of the fighting. After the Tet offensive and during Nixon's Administration the United States began pulling troops out of Vietnam and providing military assistance to South Vietnam—bringing the United States back to where it started. In the end, as we all know, the North swallowed up the South in an embarrassing defeat to the United States. Therefore, when Americans hear talk about training Iraqi troops to be responsible for their own security it should frighten us as this was the same tatic used during the Vietnam war. The only real difference is that the Iraqi insurgents do not have a country like China or Russia supporting them as the North Vietnamese did. However, the insurgents have a plethora of fanatics throughout the Middle East and could attain the power of oil through coup-de-tats. Furthermore, there is evidence that governments and individual citizens from countries such as Saudi Arabia, Iran and Syria support some terrorist groups.

From the left, all we hear is "set a deadline" which eerily sounds too much like retreat—we cannot set a deadline as it will only indicate to the insurgents that they can wait it out, gather strength and attack when the United States leaves.

America is still, however, left with the questions of securing Iraq and rebuilding the country amid a torrent of insurgent activity. I will try to answer these questions within the pages of this book.

Removal of Troops without Complete Victory

America cannot simply train a few hundred thousand Iraqi's troops and leave the country proclaiming victory. The United States must ensure the Iraqi people prosper and are free. It would be immoral for the United States to leave the country without first ensuring that at the absolute minimum all damage done to the country due to American confrontation is repaired. It is possible for the United States to train a few hundred thousand troops and leave the country proclaiming victory, but what kind of victory will America have achieved? America will leave behind a country still in chaos and a suffering people; perhaps even more so than under Saddam Hussein. How far can free elections and an established Constitution take the people of Iraq if unemployment runs rampant and the average Iraqi citizen cannot put food on the table of his/her starving children? Democracy means absolutely, nothing, nada, zip, zero to a person who is starving or a parent forced to helplessly watch his/her newborn die of dysentery, cholera, typhoid, etc, etc. What good are free elections and a Constitution when Iraq must now deal with an insurgency and/or Civil War? From this point, forward it should be established that victory cannot be proclaimed in Iraq until the people of Iraq enjoy a better standard of living than they did under Saddam Hussein. America has seen the emergence of democracies throughout the world, but most of those democracies are but a satire of what we have in the United States. If America does not help build Iraq into a prosperous nation then the lives and billions of dollars spent in Iraq will have been in vain as Iraq, with the United States completely gone, may revert back to a dictatorship. If Iraq returns to dictatorship will the United States return to Iraq to fight an army only a few years earlier it trained and armed?

Another foreseeable consequence of simply training Iraqi troops to secure the country is that American will be compelled to provide Iraq, for what could be decades, with military and financial assistance. Between the years of 1973–1979, my mother lived in the United States while my siblings and I lived in El Salvador. My mother did not forget us. She sent money to my alcoholic father so he could provide for our keep. I am not sure how much money my mom sent but I do remember my dad patiently waiting for the checks to arrive from "Los Estados Unidos." Aside from a little bit of food, a mattress made from rags, and a leaky roof, I don't ever recall benefiting much from any of the monies sent by my mother. The Iraqi people will never see the fruit of financial aid sent by the United States. Poverty and the hatred and resentment it breeds will continue in the hearts and minds of the Iraqi people. For proof of this Americans must look at how much financial aid is provided by the United States and other developed nations to third world countries; yet poverty in these countries amid the millions in aid, continuous to be rampant. The few at the top line their pockets with the foreign aid while the masses starve.

Anyone who has traveled to a foreign country knows how inexpensive things can be. When I was in El Salvador, I treated six cousins to a bountiful dinner. The price tag for the meals, including drinks was a whopping 10 U.S. Dollars. Labor in El Salvador is relatively inexpensive as well; which would explain the cost of living. One of my cousins is a middle school teacher. She earns a monstrous 100.00 dollars per month. Assuming all things being equal with 100 million dollars I could probably turn the El Salvadoran educational system into one of the best in the world. The problem here is that most of the money donated by developed nations seldom trickles down to the people.

There are those who will dismiss this book as amateur and/or silly. Well, they are probably right. With their critique, however, I fully expect a sound innovative strategy to winning (and by winning I mean leaving a prosperous and free Iraq behind) and ending the war in Iraq is put forward. Any fool can find flaws in another person's thinking or logic but its takes a special fool to come up with innovative solutions to complex problems.

Below is a 5-step plan to winning the war in Iraq. The trick is that all the steps must be done in conjunction. No step can be left behind as it will cause the others to falter.

1. Galvanize the American people behind a solid and comprehensive plan and dedicate a respectable portion of America's military, economic, industrial and technological strength to winning the war in Iraq in 2-5 years.

2. Stop the infiltration of insurgents into Iraq from Saudi Arabia, Syria and Iran. (To name a few)

3. Increase the total number of American troops to 250,000 in order to train Iraqis to secure the country.

4. Strengthen and train the Iraqi Police—If policing are the only jobs that exist now make sure those jobs pay well.

5. Quadruple reconstruction Efforts

2

GALVANIZE

Galvanize the American people behind a solid comprehensive plan and dedicate a respectable portion of America's military, economic, industrial and technological strength to winning the war in Iraq.

Does anyone in America, aside from the families of servicemen in Afghanistan and Iraq, realize we are at war? At a Memorial Day and Fourth of July party, I attended no one bothered to remember our Military personnel in harms way or even the two concurrent wars being fought by America. I wanted to stand up on a table and scream, "Don't you people realize we are at war?" Yes, we are at war. It sure does not feel like it. During World War II, rationing of food, metal and other commodities was common. Americans were encouraged to plant Victory Gardens and to buy war bonds. When was the last time you bought a war bond? And how is your "Victory Garden" coming along? If you answered, "What's a victory garden then America is indeed in dire straits. In order to ship more food products to the soldiers overseas the American government encouraged its citizen to plan victory gardens. The logic was that if you could grow your own food then you would not need to buy food and thus more food would go to American and Allied forces. To fight a war you need money so America sold "War Bonds" The war bonds where used to build new tanks, planes, submarines, machine guns, etc, etc. Since September 11, 2001 how many war bonds have you purchased or been put up for sale by the government? The point I am trying to get to is that aside from a few people driving around with American flags draping from their pick up trucks most people have forgotten we are at war.

After September 11, 2001, millions upon millions of Americans had an American flag draping from their car. As I drove down I-95, it was a site to behold. Every other car had an American flag waving. I remember the patriotic songs played constantly on the radio. Some of those songs inspired me to love America more than I already did. I remember driving down the Florida Turnpike shedding tears of pride as the patriotic tunes played at full volume in my car. I do not do that anymore.

I also remember the increase in young Americans willing to join the military. Times where so good for recruiters they turned old men like me (I am 35) away. Now that the military has failed to meet, quotas (Even after old men like me are welcomed to join-The recruitment age for the Army National Guard has increased to 39) and even the Marines have missed their recruiting goals. Can you believe that? I remember a time when there was a 9 month waiting period to join the Marines. The Few, The Proud, the Marines can't find a few recruits? During World War II hundreds of thousand of young men flooded recruiting stations throughout the United States. A typical song of the day was,

> Johnnie, get your gun, get your gun, get your gun,
> Take it on the run, on the run, on the run,
> Hear them calling you and me, ev'ry son of liberty
> Hurry right away, no delay, go today
> Make your Daddy glad to have had such a lad,
> Tell your sweetheart not to pine, to be proud her boy's in line

> Over there, over there!
> Send the word, send the word, over there!
> That the Yanks are coming, the Yanks are coming,
> The drums rum-tumming ev'rywhere!
> So prepare, say a prayer, send the word, send the word to beware!
> We'll be over, we're coming over,
> And we won't come back 'til it's over Over There!

> Johnnie, get your gun, get your gun, get your gun,
> Johnnie show the Hun you're a son of a gun!
> Hoist the flag and let her fly,
> Yankee Doodle do or die
> Pack your little kit, show your grit, do your bit

> Yankees to the ranks from the towns and the tanks
> Make your mother proud of you and the old Red White and Blue

> Over there, over there,
> Send the word, send the word, over there!

That the Yanks are coming, the Yanks are coming,
The drums rum-tumming ev'ry where
So prepare, say a prayer, send the word, send the word to beware
We'll be over, we're coming over,
And we won't come back 'til it's over Over There!

I have heard some of my elders say that if during World War II you were of fighting age and fit to fight and if you were still in the States people looked at you with disdain. It seems to me that during World War II it was unpatriotic to not be in the Military.

Now, here we are at the threshold of a new World War. I say this because the war on terror can easily turn into a world war because as soon as Iran acquires nuclear weapons the entire political and military spectrum of the Middle East will change. A Nuclear Iran, with its Mullahs in power can be very dangerous. Americans should remember that during the Cold War a nuclear war did not occur between America and Russia because the leaders of both nations knew that an attack on the other would assure mutual annihilation. Hence, the leaders of Russia and the United States knew that everybody, including the lives of those they held to be precious, would perish. The deaths in a nuclear exchange would no longer be of some unknown poor white kid from Nashville, Tennessee or a Black kid from Harlem, New York or a Latino kid from the Bronx, as it was in Vietnam. Now, even in a minor exchange of 100–300 nuclear warheads everyone would die or be left to roam a dying uninhabitable planet. The Mullahs of Iran however believe that they would be dying for Allah and become martyrs. They have proven repeatedly that they do not have a problem with suicide missions (especially if they aren't the ones actually performing the deed). Furthermore, if the mullahs know of impending nuclear strike against the United States they will move to have their love ones live in other countries. Therefore, while the United States has alot to lose the Mullahs do not and that makes them extremely dangerous.

A nuclear strike in the United States would be imminent once Iran acquires nuclear weapons. It would no longer be a matter of if but when a City like New York, Chicago or Washington would experience a nuclear attack. As it is proven every single hour of every single day in America, getting tons of cocaine and illegal drugs into the United States is not difficult at all. If it were there would not be so many drugs on America's streets. It should therefore be fully expected that terrorist, possibly in cahoots with drug lords, will smuggle a nuclear warhead or materials to assemble a nuclear warhead into the United States. It is important to remember that an atomic bomb the size of a suitcase can weald enough power to cause as much damage as the bombs dropped on Hiroshima and Nagasaki.

The affects of an atomic bomb detonated in Times Square

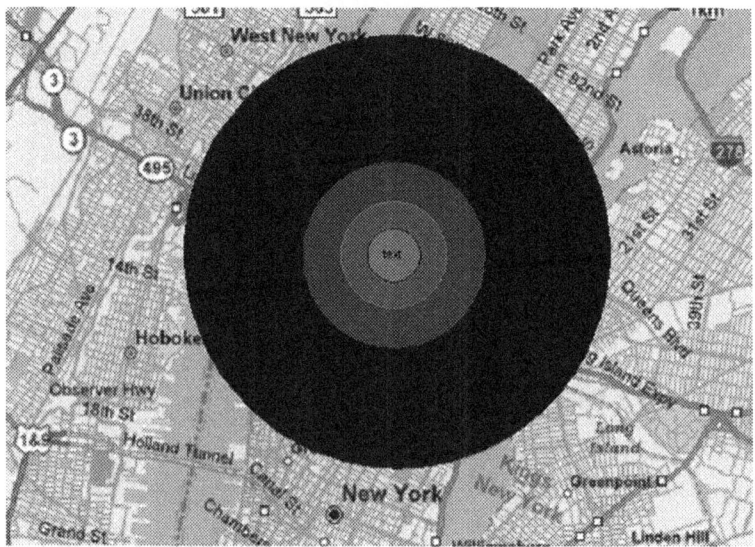

The First Circle of Death

A single atomic bomb, as the one dropped on Hiroshima on August 6, 1945, upon detonation in Time Square, New York, will probably have a kill ratio of 100% within a ½ mile radius of the epicenter. Essentially concluding everyone within the first circle will die instantly. Due to the extreme heat at the core, some 300,000 degrees, anything combustible such as cars, people, concrete, and glass or anything not made to withstand temperatures hotter than the Sun's surface, will simply be incinerated. The remains of any loves ones within this first circle will never be found. Buildings within the first circle of death will simply be blown to smithereens. The intense heat will crystallize concrete—meaning concrete will turn into billions of pieces of glass tearing through the air like billions of small bullets. Nothing, absolutely nothing will remain within the first circle of death. By the time the blast is over all of Time Square will have been reduced to rubble and a few areas will smolder.

The Second Circle of Death

Anything within the second circle, half mile to 1 mile from the epicenter will immediately catch fire; people will be burned beyond recognition. The force of the blast 10–15 PSI (Pound per Square inch) will violently tear at the foundations of all buildings forcing most of these structures to collapse under the extreme pressure. The thousands of car, trucks and buses filled with gasoline and diesel fuel within the second circle of death will only add to the inferno. Much as the steal supporting the twin towers weakened to the strength of butter, the buildings steal casing within the second circle will begin to melt. With fires, raging and building collapsing it is doubtful anyone within the second circle will survive the blast. The kill ratio for the second circle will be somewhere within 95 and 100%. Those who do survive will eventually die from smoke inhalation, severe burns or traumatic injuries such as crush bones, severed limbs and/or internal injuries.

Third Circle of Death

At 1 mile, the blast will continue unabated in its path of destruction; though the heat will be less intense. Nevertheless, the outward explosion will cause concrete to be ripped from buildings and a rain of broken glass will descend to the street below, killing and maiming anyone caught in the open. Some buildings will be able to withstand the blast but most of those buildings will be rendered useless. Most sections of the buildings-the sections facing the blast will catch fire. People caught in the open and in sight of the blast will suffer 2nd–3rd degree burns on exposed parts of the body, faces, hands, necks, ears and head. Most cars will be tossed into the air and explode causing a chain reaction until the streets of midtown Manhattan are engulfed in flames. Trapped in burning buildings people will be forced jump to their deaths or be burned alive. The kill ratio within the third circle will probably be between 80–85%. Most of the injured unless evacuated immediately will probably die within the first hour of the initial blast.

Fourth Circle of Death

Within the fourth circle, people will continue to perish, though the kill ratio will be approximately 50–65%. Those facing the blast will surely suffer some 1st and 2nd degree burns. (First and 2nd degree burn are as or as severe as bad sunburn or bulging blisters on the skin) Those unfortunate ones to see the initial flash will be blinded permanently as the cornea of the eyes will suffer irreversible damage. The blast will continue outward and most of the damage will be from excessive wind.

Old buildings will probably collapse from excessive strain while most windows will be broken injuring the occupants inside.

At this point, the blast will be less than a minute old, yet over 1 million people will be dead and hundreds upon thousands will be injured. The injuries sustained by the survivors, if they survive longer than a few days, will be life altering. After the bombs were dropped on Hiroshima and Nagasaki the people in close proximity to the blast suffered all kinds of horrific wounds:

The Mushroom cloud

A mushroom cloud will rise from Manhattan Island. It will be visible from up to 150 miles away. That is as far away as Pennsylvania, the Catskill Mountains in upstate New York, New London, Connecticut and Riverhead, Long Island. The Mushroom cloud will rise from the epicenter carrying with it deadly particles of radiation that depending on the winds can be carried as far as California or Europe. The cloud will precipitate what is referred to as Black rain. Black rain is radioactive material carried to the Atmosphere during the initial blast by the mushroom cloud, which descends back to earth far outside the fourth circle of death. This radioactive material will cause a high level of cancer occurrences to people living within several hundred miles of the epicenter (commonly referred to as "Ground Zero") for years to come.

The Immediate Aftermath

Because most communications systems will go down immediately in New York City and Manhattan is a central hub for televised communications throughout the U.S. and the World, the enormity of what has occurred will not reach Americans and the world for a few minutes. In that time most of central Manhattan will burn uncontrollably and buildings that withstood the blast will begin collapsing from the weaken structures.

Outside the fourth circle, chaos will ensue as people try and evacuate Manhattan. With such devastation and fire engulfing mid-Manhattan an organized exodus from the island seems very unlikely. Many more people will die or be injured from the onslaught of people trying to leave a burning Manhattan. More agile and able people will probably trample the elderly, handicapped or people with special needs. Within days after the blast most injured people not evacuated within several miles of ground zero will begin to die from radiation related illnesses. For several days after the blast Manhattan will burn uncontrollably as it will be impossible to get emergency crews through mountain high debris littered streets. A dark cloud will hover over the city from countless tons of radioactive smoke.

Although much of downtown (South of 23rd Street) and uptown (North of 81st Street) Manhattan will remain intact, the infrastructure to support it will be non-existent. It will not be possible to do business on the entire island for what could be a decade. Therefore, it will probably take years for the stock market to open in lower Manhattan. (An emergency trading center should be built somewhere in the country—but that's another book). As the day wears on the initial shock to the country will be many times greater than that of 9/11. Americans will demand retaliation against our enemies and in their haste our leaders will want to retaliate but the question of the day will be, "Who do we retaliate against?" America will have no choice but to respond with massive nuclear strikes against Iran and North Korea. Nuclear strike against these two foes will not go without colossal protest from Russia and China. However, their protest will be nothing compared to the unrest that will be spawned throughout the Muslim world.

The Economy after the Blast

The stock market in The United States, when it reopens, will probably lose all gains since inception. If the loses after the 9/11 are to serve as a gauge, we must remember that after market opened, only 4 days after the attacks, it lost over 700 points within the first days of trading. Therefore, it would probably be prudent for the markets to stay closed for as long as possible in order for investors to fully understand and measure the economic blow sustained. A nuclear blast in a city like New York City, even as severe as one would be, still would not destroy the American economy, but the fear it will spawn can and will destroy the stock market. Most world markets will probably follow suit. Losses this catastrophic will plunge America and the world into a deep depression. Millions and millions of jobs will be lost, along with the retirement savings of millions upon millions more. The economic losses will be in the trillions of dollars.

The economic loses will extend throughout the world. Countries like China, Germany, France, Russia and most of the world can bet they will lose their wealthiest customer for at least a few years as the American economy will plummet and America will stop the import of all goods into the United States. Just as the United States grounded all flight for 3 days after the 9/11 attacks, exporters to America can bet no imports coming into the United States will be accepted. Countries like China, Germany and France—some of America's biggest suppliers of goods will suffer devastating losses to their economies and their multi-million-aires will probably lose millions upon millions. It must be clear that America will not be the only loser after such a devastating attack. Therefore, it is in the best interest of all nations; especially America's biggest importers of goods to ensure Iran and North Korea or any other rogue nations do not proclaim "Nuclear Power" status.

In the Wake

Iran and North Korea will likely launch pre-emptive strikes after news of the atomic detonation in New York—It will be the old "use them or lose them" mentality. North Korea will probably annihilate Japan and South Korea. Iran will probably launch strikes against Israel and the closes American military installation—Baghdad; though Baghdad may escape simply because it is a Muslim Capitol—but I doubt the Mullahs will be persuaded by the qur'an which teaches Muslim should not kill Muslims—though it doesn't seem to stop them from killing innocent Muslims everyday (But that too is another book). Twenty-Four hours after the atom explosion in Manhattan, Iran and North Korea will probably not exist but Kim Young Il his family member and prominent members of Iran's Mullahs and their families will almost certainly be alive and well somewhere in the world. Meanwhile over 1 billion Muslims will be convinced that America has declared war on all Muslims. In protest, OPEC may stop all oil imports to the United States plunging America deeper into economic ruin.

Hurricane Katrina

I did not want to write about Hurricane Katrina because I did not wish to politicize such a horrendous natural disaster. However, it is important for Americans to fully understand what the lack of response truly means. If Hurricane Katrina is to serve as a gauge for America's preparedness to deal with a nuclear strike or any strike with WMDs then we must surmise the lack of response to the humanitarian crisis which would ensue after a nuclear attack upon a major American city. Failure to respond in the aftermath of Hurricane Katrina was at the Local, State and Federal level. All governmental institutions had ample warning from the National Hurricane Center in Miami of the potential for destruction in New Orleans, Mississippi and Alabama due to Hurricane Katrina. As of the writing of this book, September 7, 2005, finger pointing has begun. However, the blame lies squarely with all facets of the government. Neither George W. Bush, Congress, New Orleans Mayor Nagin nor Government Blanco share sole responsibility for the failure to execute upon their oath. They all share equal culpability for utter failure and the American people must hold them accountable for the entire fiasco. Even 4 years after 9/11 and billions spent on Homeland security America is still unprepared to deal with a major catastrophe; whether natural or man made. Therefore, as Manhattan burns in the aftermath of a nuclear detonation, the American people, unless procedures and preparedness are rectified, can fully expect the government will be unable to aid anyone on Manhattan Island. Hence, Americans can fully expect a death toll in the millions.

Point to consider

On September 11, 2001, I witnessed the twin towers fall with shear horror and helplessness. As the days wore on, and the enormity of what had occurred dawned upon me, I forced my self to find a silver lining in the ashes arising from the smoldering Twin Towers, but I could not find any. After experiencing the long lines at the airports and the tight security, I thought to myself. "I wonder if the drugs lords of the world will be angry and start eliminating terrorist organizations because now it will be very difficult for them to get their drugs into the United States." I was so wrong—drugs keep pouring into the Unites States as if it was excess social security money…While little old ladies, women with babies are harassed and beautiful women are lusciously padded down at the airports our ports and borders remain ever so porous. Hundreds of pounds of cocaine and other illegal drugs pour into the country each and every day. And that is how they will get the materials to assemble a nuclear bomb into the Unite States.

It is important to return back to how America was galvanized after the attacks on Pearl Harbor. For four years, the entire country threw itself into fighting and winning the war in Europe and in the Pacific. Franklin D. Roosevelt did a splendid job—even without the Internet and 24 hour news channels—to hardness the power of the American people behind a specific goal. And he did it without setting a deadline. Everyone knew the war needed to be won and that was the focus. I cannot begin to imagine what kind of a world we would live in today if America had not won the war against Axis powers. Conceivably, as a Hispanic, I would probably not be writing this book. As for Caucasians not of blond hair and blue eyes, you would probably be servants to those with blond hair and blue eyes.

Our leaders in Washington must galvanize the entire country into winning the war on terror. The President must go on television, clearly explain the dangers we face and plainly outline the steps we must take to eliminate those dangers. The war in Iraq cannot be won by only military and political means. We must win the war by rebuilding the entire country of Iraq. And we can win by harnessing the power of the American people.

What are the Dangers we face?

- A failed Iraq will create more enemies not only in the Middle East but also throughout the world.

- America will surely face more attacks; attacks even on our own soil.

- A failed Iraq will surely propel the Iranians into harnessing their nuclear ambitions.

- A failed Iraq will weaken America

- A failed Iraq will put our allies in grave danger

- A failed Iraq will dissolve the hard won accomplishments achieved to date; like Libya abandoning its nuclear ambitions, elections in Iraq, Lebanon and Saudi Arabia

- A failed Iraq will surely cause the price of Oil to skyrocket as American will seem weak and at the mercy of Oil Producing Nations.

A failed Iraq will create more enemies throughout the Middle East and the world

If the United States fails in Iraq her enemies will know that in order to defeat the United States all you need is a few thousand-suicide bombers and some patience. As we have seen on television, Pakistan alone has thousands upon thousands of these volunteers waiting in the wings. A failure in Iraq will only spur many, many more. Throughout the world, there are hundreds of organizations that hate the United States. Indonesia, Thailand, Pakistan, Saudi Arabia, Syria, Libya, Somalia to name a few, host thousands of terrorist groups just eager to kill Americans and to give up their lives for Allah.

America will surely face more attacks

A failure in Iraq will give our enemies the impression that we are at our weakest point and they will use that weakness to attack us. Our enemies may even be so bold as to try and attack us militarily on our own soil. As absurd as this may sound if I had stood in Central park on September 10, 2001 and told you that by the next day the Twin Towers would be gone, you would not have believed me and I would have probably been arrested for disturbing the peace. Therefore, do not under-estimate the resolve of our enemies. Although I will admit that, a military attack on our own soil is highly unlikely; a terrorist attack or two isn't!

A failed Iraq will surely propel the Iranians into harnessing their nuclear ambitions

Even as I write, the Iranians are diligently working on their "peaceful" nuclear program. (Why would a country with 25% or more of oil reserves in the world need a nuclear reactor—that is like Eskimos needing an icemaker?) A failure in Iraq will probably make the Mullahs of Iran more brazen in their pursuit of nuclear weapons. If anyone thinks the Mullahs will not let one of their bombs "accidentally" disappear is kidding themselves. The Mullahs will help our enemies acquire nuclear weapons. And terrorist will be more than happy to deliver the bomb to any city in America—COD.

A failed Iraq will weaken America

After America was defeated in Vietnam, the mood around the country was somber. When Ronald Reagan won election in 1980 the military, though still formidable was not anywhere near what it is today or it was after World War II and the Korean War. Even the Stock Market during the 1970's went through a period of less than desirable growth. In 1966, the Dow hit an all time high of 995.15. In 1982, the Dow was in the 800's. Inflation was rampant and who could forget the oil embargo. In the mid 1970's the country was still trying to absorb the expenditure of over 600 billions dollars to fight the war in Vietnam, accommodate 153,000 combat wounded service personnel and recover from an embarrassing defeat. In whole, a defeat in Iraq will plunge the country into a depressed state—anyone would be depressed after getting whipped by a smaller opponent. Just look at Mike Tyson during his last fight. It was pitiful to watch him sit there and say he fell like a 100 year old man.

A failed Iraq will put our allies in danger

Spain withdrew its military forces from Iraq even after the Madrid bombings. This was a clear victory for the terrorist. Every time a coalition partner withdraws it troops the terrorist get a major victory. If America is to fail in Iraq, Spain, France, England and Germany can surely expect terrorist attacks of their own. This is a guarantee as terrorists pray on fear. Over the years, we have come to know why Germany and France decided to stay out of the fight in Iraq. They had other interest in Iraq before the war and they wanted to protect those interest.

The old adage, "Money talk's bullshit walks" is completely and utterly true in this case. To engage the Germans and French the United States must allow them to take part in the lucrative rebuilding contracts now available in Iraq. But this is outside the scope of my point. My point here is that if America fails in Iraq our allies can definitely expect terrorist attacks. The fact remains that pound for pound the terrorist probably have more respect for America than for Germany, Spain and France because at least we are willing to fight! I know growing up in the ghetto; I always had more respect for the guy whom I knew was willing to fight me than for the guy who cowered in my presence.

A failed Iraq will dissolve the hard won accomplishments achieved to date: Libya abandoning its nuclear ambition, elections in Iraq, Lebanon and Saudi Arabia

Some countries in the Middle East have come to see the great promise in Democracy and freedom for all. Libya has given up its nuclear ambitions and that is wonderful. Perhaps now instead of spending 1 billion dollars to acquire nuclear weapons Col. Muammar al-Qaddafi will channel that money towards improving the lives of his people. Recently the government of Lybia announced it would be buying laptops for all its school age children

Almost 3000 American service men and women have died in Iraq. Those men and women paid the ultimate sacrifice in order to give the Iraqi people the opportunity to vote. Thankfully, the Iraqi people have bravely taken advantage of the opportunity afforded to them. They elected a government and look to it with hope. A failure in Iraq will be a disgrace to those who have already died and those who have yet to do so. In Saudi Arabia, elections have been held and in Lebanon, elections were held just a few months ago. Now, would these elections have occurred without the guidance of the United States? Well, probably not. Is the road to democracy all but completed in the Middle East? No, absolutely not. The road to democracy is long and arduous. The seeds of democracy where planted by the Greeks and to this day Democracy continues to evolve. We cannot therefore expect overnight Democracy in the Middle East. It is, however, vital for the world to see that Democracy flourishes and that it becomes the synthesis to a better form of government. Who knows what new form of government lies ahead?

A failed Iraq will surely cause the price of Oil to skyrocket as American will seem weak and at the mercy of Oil Producing Nations

A failed Iraq will most definitely plunge Iraq into a long and bloody civil war. That civil war may even draw some of its neighbors into the fight. In todays, market just the mere mention of any kind of oil disruption sends the price of crude through the roof. Therefore, a failed Iraq will surely make the price of oil rise.

Before I continue, I want to discuss America's dependence on Foreign Oil. It is probably prudent to acknowledge that America, while importing over 60% of the petroleum it uses, is already at the mercy of OPEC. Even the current U.S. President, with great "friends" in Saudi Arabia has failed to get the price of oil to drop below 45 dollars per barrel. It is important for U.S. Citizen to realize that OPEC can easily manipulate our entire way of life. If OPEC decided to cut off all imports to the United States, America would come to an almost complete halt in less than 2 months. Our dependence on OPEC is, at best, extremely dangerous to our National Security. During the Oil Embargo of the mid 70's, gas lines stretched for miles and gas was rationed in the United States. In the 1970s, America imported less than 50% of its oil from the Middle East; yet, the oil embargo caused severe pain at the pumps. It is therefore absolutely necessary for the people of the United States to fully explore the effects another oil embargo would have in the year 2005 and beyond.

Other Unforeseen Consequences

There are probably many more maladies that can come from the United States failing in Iraq but I simply want to make the point here that we cannot fail in Iraq as immediate consequences are clear and the unknown ones are terrifying. The merits for going to war in Iraq may be debatable but winning is not.

Galvanize America

There isn't a nation on this earth that can militarily, economically or technologically defeat the United States and remain standing after doing so. The American people have the power to force its government to achieve any goal. In the 1960's, President Kennedy galvanized the American people into putting a man on the moon and it was done! Americans have built the most extensive road structure in the history of the world. Americans propel a multi-trillion dollar economy every day of their lives. If Americans wanted to, they could land a person on Mars and return, him/her back to earth safely within a decade. As Americans we posses great power, we as a people have the military, economical and industrial strength to bring any country to its knees in a matter of weeks, even days. As Americans, we posses the power to at the very least temporarily annihilate the economy of any country by simply boycotting its products.

What we do not posses is a leader to guide us and to motivate us to achieve the unachievable. Our current leaders are not motivating us to win a war. No one can dispute that at home we have a lot of issues we need to address. We all must worry about our mortgages/rent, putting our children in school, healthcare, etc, etc. I understand all of that. I am too worried about how I am going to pay my mortgage when my savings run out. I am worry about my daughter's lack of healthcare coverage since I lost my job. I am, however, more worried about losing a war, about Iran acquiring nuclear weapons and someday turning on the news to find New York City or Washington D.C. no longer exists. If 9/11 caused an economic downturn, which took almost 2 years to recover from, what can America expect from nuclear attack? How long will it take the American economy to recover from such devastation? The real priority here is to win the war in Iraq as quickly and decisively as possible. The longer we are bogged down in Iraq the less likely we are to win simply by virtue that we cannot continue the current expenditure forever.

It is therefore imperative for the United States government to galvanize the American people into winning the war in Iraq. As mentioned at the beginning of this book America must devote a great portion of its economical, industrial, technological and military might into winning the war in Iraq. It must all begin with the American people.

How can the U.S. government galvanize the American people?

1. Explain to the American people how the war will be won and continue giving updates on the progress or lack thereof.

2. Encourage all Americans to buy war bonds

3. Ration building materials and any other items deemed necessary to win the war in Iraq.

4. Initiate a massive recruiting effort to fill the ranks of our military

5. Continue explaining to the American people the consequences of losing the war

6. Form a military Division comprised mostly of American Muslims

7.   Encourage all Americans into contributing to the war effort.

8.   Dedicate a cable channel to news about the war in Iraq

9.   Devise a campaign that will keep the American people tuned into the progress of the war

Explain to the American people how the war will be won and continue giving updates on the progress or lack thereof

For starters, the President must go on television and advise the American people of his plan to win the war in Iraq within a period of 2–5 years. After he has explained his method for winning the war, the President must call for the people of the United States to join him in the struggle. He must convince the American people that for the next few years, Americans will have to endure some hardships as some materials and technology will be diverted towards the rebuilding of Iraq. In his speech, the President must enumerate the dangers and consequences of losing the war in Iraq and he must explain to the American people why it is vital for us to rebuild Iraq and win the war as quickly as possible. The President must call on all young men and women of fighting age to consider joining the military and he must have his daughters at his side. He must be willing to have his own children fight in this war. After getting the approval of the American people, the President must hold weekly news conferences explaining to the American people the progress and setbacks suffered in Iraq. The President must continue to try and galvanize the America people throughout all of his weekly speeches.

Encourage all Americans to buy war bonds

Because adding 100,000 troops and rebuilding Iraq will increase the daily price tag in Iraq, the United States must sell war bonds and encourage all Americans to buy them. Obviously, money raised through the sale of war bonds will add much needed capital to the rebuilding efforts in Iraq. A prosperous Iraq may lead to lower oil prices and greater economic growth in the United States and around the world.

Ration building materials and any other items deemed necessary to win the war in Iraq.

This will be a tough one for America to swallow because of the current boom in housing throughout the United States. However, I am quite certain that through tax incentives and other forms of enticements the U.S. government can convince manufacturers of steal, air conditioning units, lumber and other building materials to increase their output. Americans may for a short while need to curb their need for large, luxurious housing but in the end, after Iraq has been rebuilt, American manufacturing and building industries will have the capacity to continue with the housing boom. Of course, a side benefit with increased output will be the creation of jobs in America and help the American economy. I also believe that a focused leadership to rebuilding Iraq will spawn and entire industry and thus propelling the American economy forward.

Initiate a massive recruiting effort to fill the ranks of our military

The United States of America must unfortunately increase the size of its military or shift American firepower from areas where we are no longer needed, such as Germany. However, it is probably prudent that America build a military force capable of fighting three or more wars. Therefore, the U.S. government must increase the size of its military by at least 250,000 troops. If Americans are fully aware of the danger posed by a nuclear Iran and North Korea, it will not be necessary to entice America's young and brave to join the military with potentially unaffordable bonuses. America's young men and women will join because the country needs them. On a side note, our congressional leaders must also be willing to let their children of combat age serve in the military. Americans must see that the challenges facing America are so grave that even our leaders are willing to send their children into harm's way. It is imperative for the United States to prepare to fight to protect Israel from aggressive Middle Eastern nations. As we have already seen, some of our allies cannot be relied upon to help us fight any wars and therefore we must be prepared to fight several foes on our own.

Continue explaining to the American people the consequences of losing the war

Unlike most people throughout the world Americans, have extremely busy lives. Our jobs demand more and more of our time each year. Many Americans are workaholics. Due to our frantic lives, we cannot be expected to worry about conflicts happening thousands of miles away. Perhaps that is why the flag no longer waves as it did after the 9/11 attacks. As shocked as the country was we got over the initial shock and continued on with the problems we face each day. Therefore, the war in Iraq must be kept at the forefront of our minds or it will be brought to our doorstep once more. The President must continuously galvanize the American people into supporting the war through speeches and reminders as to why we need to win.

Form a military Division comprised mostly of American Muslim Fighting men and women

Of all the recommendations I have listed in this book this one if probably the most controversial. It sounds too much like the "blacks" only units of World War II. During World War II "Black" units were simply created to keep black and white troops separated. The creation of a mostly Muslim division will be for the purposes of demonstrating to the Muslim world that America and her allies wish to demonstrate a gesture of good will towards Iraqis and the Middle East. This type of gesture may further demonstrate that America simply wishes to share with Iraq the same blessings of democracy we so apathetically enjoy. There are somewhere between 5–8 million Muslims living in the United States. The United States must form a division of mostly Muslim Americans to serve as a transitional Army after most U.S. troops has left Iraq. This division although military should consist of mostly young men and women trained at policing and relief personnel. In other words this, "army" should serve almost as the Peace Corps serves throughout the world today.

Encourage all Americans into contributing to the war effort.

Our leaders in Washington and local government must encourage every American to contribute whatever they can to the war effort. The contribution can range from letter writing campaigns to American service personnel to the direct communication between American citizens and Iraqis. At no time in world history has this been easier to do this than today.

Dedicate a cable channel to news about the war in Iraq

A cable channel dedicated to bringing news from Iraq should be dedicated and made available to every major metropolitan area in the United States. Said channel should be allowed to broadcast any story it wishes with the exception, of course, of military tactics or anything hindering the effectiveness of the military's ability to fight.

Devise a campaign that will keep the American people tuned into the progress of the war

A bipartisan political campaign must be devised to keep the American people involved and tuned into the progress of the war. The President must continue to keep the support of the American people as it is his greatest asset.

The point being made here is that a war cannot be won without the support of the American people. As it is commonly known the Vietnam War was not lost by

American fighting forces. At every military engagement in Vietnam, our military forces soundly defeated their opponents. The war was lost not in the jungles of Vietnam but rather on streets of Washington, D.C. and university and college campuses. Therefore, it is vital for the President and Congress to get the support and approval of the American people or this war will be lost. America cannot afford to lose the war in Iraq. The consequences of losing will be devastating. Therefore, it is vital, absolutely vital for Americans to collectively fight and win. The President must galvanize American into mustering all of its energy into rebuilding Iraq economically, politically and militarily.

A Short Story

On March 29, 2003, I was on a flight headed to from Fort Lauderdale to New York. I had just finished a major project with Walt Disney World and I had recently been offered a great job with another company. So, having spent 6 months working extremely long hours, I decided to take a week's vacation before starting my new job. At the time, I had not taken a trip alone with my daughter in a few months so I decided I would bring my little girl, whom at the time was 21 months old, to New York with me. I am accustomed to taking her with me to the mall, parks and the beach so I packed all of her belongings, put her in one those back packs designed to carry babies and toddlers and headed off to the air-port. The trip to the airport was uneventful. Because she was still under 2 years old, I did not have to buy a ticket for her so she simply sat on my lap. Naturally, my daughter is the most beautiful child in the world so it wasn't a surprise to me that everyone on the plane commented on her utter cuteness—just like her dad...As a proud father and thanked them for their kind and overly obvious sin-cere words. My daughter and I sat on an aisle seat. I chose an aisle seat in case I needed to change her diaper, I would do so without disturbing other passengers. The lady next to me and I made small talk. She was a very pleasant woman who was going to New York to visit her sick mother and spend a few moments with family members. The plane took off without any problems and we were at cruis-ing altitude when I heard a passenger raise his voice. With 9/11 still vivid on everyone's mind the entire plane grew quiet until only the noise of the plane's engines could be heard. From my aisle seat, I could see a male flight attendant standing over a passenger. They were sitting about 12 rows from my daughter and me so I could not make out their conversation. Suddenly the passenger stood up. At that point, I knew something terrible was about to happen. I handed my daughter to the lady sitting next to me and unfastened my seatbelt. The passen-

ger's agitation with the flight attendant only grew more intense. At this point, another flight attendant announced that there was a minor dispute taking place with a passenger and they wanted everyone to remain seated. I relaxed a bit, but no sooner had I relaxed that the passenger began pointing and screaming at the flight attendant. With a crazed look on his face, he turned around and asked for someone to help him. He yelled, "I want to get off this plane right now!" The tall Caucasian man, about 6 feet 2 inches tall, weighing 230 pounds suddenly rushed the emergency exit. I stood up and rushed to the scene to try and help the flight attendant restrain the man. Unable to open the emergency exit he turned around and with his elbow began crushing the neck of an unfortunate woman who was sitting next to the emergency exit. The flight attendant and I both started asking him to please let the woman go. He kept saying, "No one better hurt me." Meanwhile the poor woman begged us to help her. She kept crying out, "Please help me. Please help me". The belligerent man then said, "Stay away from me or I will stab her." He held his cell phone to the woman's throat as to indicate slashing. At this point it appeared to me he reached underneath the seat. So within a fraction of a second both the flight attendant and I, without any communication, seem to have agreed negotiations with the man were over. If he had a knife underneath the seat, it would spell certain death or serious injury to the woman who was now in complete hysterics. Both the flight attendant and I reached for his shirt and pulled him off of the woman. To my surprise, I remember thinking, "Wow, it was easy to pull this big guy off the woman." It wasn't until a few seconds later that I realized two football player size African-American men were behind me pulling. About five of us struggled in the aisle with the man. We were trying to subdue him by placing him on the floor of the plane, but he fought back. I remember a college age boy punching him in the face while we were trying to tie him up with belts. Another elderly man kept hitting him with something he had in his hand. All the while, I was yelling to the belligerent man to get on the ground. I clearly remember saying, "You son of a bitch—my little girl is on this flight. How dare you. Get down mother-fucker" When he refused, I placed one hand on his genitals and squeezed as hard as I could. I have often wondered how hard I must have squeezed. With my adrenaline pumping and the exertion of strength generated by anger, it must have been pretty hard. In any event, sure enough, as you may have guessed, he screeched loudly and he went down like a sack of potatoes. Once he was down, he asked for us to please let him go. He said, "You're hurting me. Let me go, I won't do that again." I said, "You should have thought about that before you started this shit." After the man was subdued, I became worried over my daughter's well being. I was now sitting on top of the man so I asked someone to take my place. There was no shortage of volunteers. I ran back to my seat to find my daughter was safe. I started crying and kissing her when I thought of what could have happened to her. I was certain my daughter would have been sucked from my arms and out of the plane had I not intervened and the belligerent man been successful at opening the emergency exit door at 37,000 feet. I kept thinking that it would have been so unfair for her to die.

The plane made an emergency landing at the Raleigh/Durham North Carolina International airport. The man and his luggage were taken off the plane and we continued our trip to New York. The captain of the plane thanked all of the passengers who had helped. The passengers cheered and heralded us as heroes. Every time I have told this story people have said, "Wow, you're a hero." Well, perhaps they are right and the feeling of being called a hero is good, but the fact is that after 9/11 I doubt any, any American would ever let a man or group of men take over a plane without a fight. I have always held that the hijackers succeeded at taking over 3 planes and crashing them into the Twin Towers and the Pentagon simply because as Americans we have always been taught to let the proper authorities take care of hostage situations. We have been taught to do what hijackers demand of us and not to confront them. From experience, however, I can tell you there is no way a group of Americans will ever let a person or group of persons take over a plane! I can almost guarantee that on any flight there will be at minimum a group of 10–20 Americans willing, ready and capable of kicking some serious ass. That poor guy on the flight to New York got his ass severely whooped and his testicles mangled. I think the next time he decides to act up he will remember what happened to his testicles.

I am telling you this story because if there are any terrorists out there thinking of hijacking a plane they should know that they will surely face fierce resistance from the Americans on board and if any of those Americans have read this book they will mangle your testicles too. And just think with mangled testicles you won't be able to do anything with those hundreds of virgins you've been promised.

3

A CLEAR STRATEGY

I think everyone reading this book knows that achieving a complex project requires, at the very least; planning, analysis and proper resource and time management. Since the war in Iraq began, I have yet to see a clear and concise project plan to win the war. The war began beautifully because apparently the guys at the Pentagon have perfected the art of blowing stuff up. Up to the moment, American troops rolled into Baghdad the war plan was executed with astounding surgical precision. There isn't a project manager or surgeon in the world who could not have been more proud. From that point on it has been as if a bunch of clowns stepped in to run the show.

First, we were told the objective was to find Weapons of Mass Destruction (WMDs). The U.N., American experts and American elite soldiers ran all over Iraq looking for WMDs. Fortunately or unfortunately, no WMDs were found; not even a few vials of stink bombs. Be that as it may, Someone in the military got a great idea to make playing cards out of the 54 most wanted men in Iraq; It was comprised of Saddam and his band of thugs. That was kind of cool, so the entire mindset shifted to finding Saddam and his band of thugs. And so Saddam was caught; he had crawled up in a little hole hiding like a frightened pathetic rat. Then all we heard about was transfer of sovereignty to the Iraqis. And everyone ran around saying, transfer of sovereignty for the Iraqis, transfer of sovereignty to the Iraqis."…Then all we heard was, "Elections, elections". As of the writing of this book, all we hear is, "Train Iraqi troops to secure the country, train Iraqi troops to secure the country.'

On June 28, 2005, the President of the United States finally went on television to outline what everyone thought would be a clear strategy to winning the war in Iraq. During the President's speech, I expected to hear a clearly delineated strategy, but all I heard was the same old rhetoric. During his 30 minute speech there was absolutely no new thinking or tactics on how America will win the war. The President praised our troops, the least of which he could do, and vehemently

38

proclaimed the war on terror is being won, without acknowledging any setbacks suffered by a coalition of the "willing". I don't know about the folks reading this book but every time someone in my life has painted a rosy picture of any situation, I have always come to find things aren't are perky as they have been made out to be…

I am not advocating the government divulge every aspect of how it will fight the war, but the government must provide the American people with a roadmap as to how we will win. At what point do we proclaim victory? Throughout my professional life at every client site, I have always developed what is referred to as the "Acceptance Criteria". This document contains a list of specific items, which must be in production and running with minimal or no malfunction before the project is considered a success. Without all of the items, specified as working as previously agreed to, the customer is not bound to pay for the software and or professional services.

Below you will find several items I believe should be in place before the United States can claim victory in Iraq. I have dubbed it "We Have Won Checklist". PLEASE NOTE: There are probably a hundred other items we can add to the "We Have Won Checklist" but for the purposes of this book, we will only stick to 21 items listed.

We have won checklist

	Items	Current Status (As of 8/30/2005)	Pass	Fail
1	Iraqi's have a constitution based on principals of democracy, religious tolerance and equal rights for all men and women.	Iraq new constitution makes Islam the basis for its doctrine and rule of law. Hardly sounds like a good constitution to me.		
2	Iraqi has a well-trained and equipped army of over 250,000 men/women and another 100,000 police officers.	Not even close.		
3	Iraq's infrastructures such as Water, Electricity, and Sanitation are working at 90% capacity with little or no interruption.	I don't think anyone knows this one.		

4	Iraq is at 99% or more of its oil production capacity. (this must be at a high percentage because this is how Iraq will pay for all it needs).	Not even close.
5	Iraq's hospitals have most if not all they need to handle the medical needs of its people.	Unknown but probably not.
6	Food distribution must be at 90% capacity.	Unknown.
7	Schools are open and moderately stocked with educational materials.	Good progress has been made here but no one really knows how much about the status of each school.
8	Unemployment rate is at or below 11%.	Not Even Close.
9	Iraq's government is adhering strictly to constitutionally mandated elections.	Yes, somewhat, hard to gauge since only 1 election has been held.
10	At least 60% of all building destroyed by America during the opening stages of the war have been rebuilt or new structures benefiting the Iraqi people have been erected. (parks, homes, schools, hospitals, etc, etc).	Unknown...no figures...at least I could not find any on the internet.
11	Saddam Hussein's palaces have been bulldozed and turned into Freedom parks for all Iraqis to enjoy.	Not Even Close.
12	50% of Baghdad's road have been repaved or repaired.	Not Even Close.
13	Life expectancy for Iraqis has increased to 3 years higher than during Saddam's reign of terror.	Not Even Close.
14	Iraqi infant mortality rate has decreased.	Terrible at best.

15	Malnourishment of Iraqi children has diminished by 25%.	Terrible at best.
16	Women have gained most if not all rights enjoyed by men.	Under Iraq's recently signed Constitution women are actually losing rights they had under Saddam Hussein.
17	All commercial flights into Baghdad have resumed.	Most countries will not fly their citizens into Iraq as of the writing of this book. This is detrimental as certain sectors of any economy depend on travelers.
18	Iraq has diplomatic relationship with almost all countries.	I am not sure. I could not find how many countries have diplomatic ties to Iraq.
19	Saddam Hussein and his henchmen have all been tried by the Iraqi people without American interference.	Not Even Close.
20	90% of insurgents have been defeated.	Going backwards instead of forward.
21	80% of all military missions are carried out by Iraqi troops with minimal U.S. supervision.	Not Even Close.

Once all of the above items receive a 'check' in the "Pass" column America can consider the war won and over. Naturally, as Iraqis assume more responsibility for the country's security American Forces can begin to withdraw slowly. It must be clear, however, to the American and Iraqi people that unless real progress is being made on all or the above items American forces will not withdraw. In other words, the logic must be as follows: "**If** Iraq assumes 80% of its military mission with minimal or no U.S. supervision **then**10,000 U.S. troops will leave the country." Each milestone must allow for the slow withdrawal of American troops. This will serve several purposes. First it will show the Iraqi people that Americans are not there to stay and second it demonstrates to all Middle Eastern nations that we are not imperialist. A gradual American withdrawal will also prove to the insurgency that America is leaving and perhaps their hatred will subside. Hence, Americans will finally see an end to the war. We can then refocus our efforts on tackling serious domestic issues plaguing our society: out of Control Health Care Cost, 45 Million Uninsured, 12.7% poverty among our own fellow Americans, 8 Trillion dollar Debt, 480 billion dollar deficit, failing Schools, Social Security Reform, dependence on Foreign Oil, etc, etc.

Now that we have established what items we need to accomplish in order to declare victory in Iraq we must formulate a plan to execute each and every item within a specific time period. Obviously, we cannot afford to keep 250,000 troops in Iraq (This is the number I am recommending for Iraq) indefinitely as it will drain our economic resources. If I were leading this project, I would hire 21 people to help me achieve each item. I would hire those persons who are professionals and renowned in each item. I would then give them the authority and money to hire all the people they need to help them accomplish their objective. My only constraint to them would be a specific time period—2–5 years. The project must be complete in 2–5 years. The 21 individuals I hire would report directly to me and I would report to the President of the United States, Congress and the American people. Each person I hired would need to provide me with a concise, well thought out plan to achieve success.

Their project plan would need to include approximate budget, personnel and resources required. Project Plans by their nature need to contain a plethora of information based on foreseeable and non-foreseeable dependencies. A good project plan attempts to foresee into the future to try and foretell what dependencies will affect the plan. For example, as the owner of item 10, I would need U.S. military protection for my workers. Therefore, without adequate protection I would not start construction. Hence, this type of dependency would be included in my plan. Naturally, I would not expect the plan to be executed perfectly but I would expect a certain level of accuracy based on what I presumed to have been thoughtful and concise development given to the plan.

I hope that by now you are starting to see where I am going with this book. I am attempting to handle the reconstruction of Iraq in a well thought out plan. This book by no means can be construed as a complete architecture of how to win the war in Iraq. What I am simply trying to do here is to provide a 50 thousand foot view of what a winning Iraqi plan should look like. I am hopeful that anyone in Washington, DC or the Pentagon reading this book will come away with at least 1 good idea or generate an original thought; though I am more afraid of backlash from people who will feel threatened by what I have written. My own mother has asked me not to publish this book because as she says, "It is too honest." Nevertheless, I love America, and if what I write will cause me to be persecuted by her; so be it. If my writings anger Muslim extremist and they declare a fatwa for my death, then they will have only proven me right and I am willing to give my life. I have no fear of death or persecution, as I have not violated God's commandment; "Thou shall not kill."

As of the writing of this book I am not sure if some of what I have already discussed is in motion. If it is then great if it is not then perhaps someone should be paying attention. If what I have suggested so far is repetitious and already being done by the U.S. government then perhaps this is the kind of information, we, the American people, should be getting from the President and our Congressional leaders

NAY Sayers

Outlining the specific goals for winning a war is not in the best interest of Washington politicians as it will force them to acknowledge defeat if and when it occurs. At the outset of the war, Americans were told that it was necessary to invade Iraq as it posed an imminent danger to our society. Americans rallied behind the President and we went to war only to find the WMDs were a figment of the President's imagination. (At the beginning of this book I mentioned WMDs could have, in a coordinated effort between Saddam Hussein's, Iran's Mullahs and Osama Bin Laden, been moved out of the Iraq but that is pure speculation grounded simply on the basis of the Iranian's hate towards America and the West.)

After WMDs were not found in Iraq, the President sold the war on several other principles. My favorite one is that we are fighting terrorists in Iraq rather than at home. On the surface, this makes sense as I would not want to fight the terrorist on American soil or with an Army of emergency relief workers. However, this argument eventually fails because America is then saying, "We do not want to fight the insurgents/terrorists here we want to fight them over there"—making the Iraqi people suffer instead of us—better them than us. At this point in time, America has said it will leave Iraqs when Iraqis have formed a Constitution, established a freely elected government and are able to secure the country. In this case, the objective of regime change is established and victory can be declared. This begs the questions, "What kind of victory will America have achieved?" And was the price tag, in both American lives and tax revenue expenditures, worth it? How will America gauge such a victory? And what if Iraq, after years of relentless insurgency, returns to dictatorship or a pseudo democracy? Will America still declare victory? Americans must demand a vision of what victory" will look like. On May 1, 2003, the President landed on the U.S.S. Abraham Lincoln and announced "Mission accomplished". The nation rallied and rejoiced at the victory we had been given. That was almost 4 years ago, over 3000 American lives and over 250 billions dollars later. Will we declare victory in Iraq during the last few years of the Bush Administration only to find America still in Iraq in 2009?

The Pentagon failed to plan for an insurgency. It should completely and utterly appall Americans to know some of the most intelligent people in the country; men who graduated from America's top rated schools like Harvard, Yale, West Point, Naval Academy and many other highly respected institutions of knowledge failed to foretell an insurgency, when insurgencies have sprouted after every invasion from any potent state. We can probably surmise the French Resistance during World War II was sprouting even as German troops paraded through Paris. Our military strategist, however, did not need to go as far back in history to know any invasion would follow an insurgency. The Afghans defeated the Soviets during the 1980s. At the onset of the Soviet invasion, they too were victorious until the Afghans banded together and started guerilla type warfare. The soviets pulled out of Afghanistan after an expenditure of billions of dollars only to face disintegration of their nation a few years later.

It is of utmost importance for America to outline clear, unambiguous objectives to winning the war in Iraq. Leaving Iraq in a state of chaos and upheaval will only further entice evildoers to perpetuate their violence on to American soil.

We have lost check list

If follows logically that if we are going to have a "We have won Checklist" we need to also have a "We Have Lost" checklist. If America had never lost a war, I would be hesitant to put this list here but since we have lost before it is necessary. Of course, these items can only be assessed after 80% of American troops have been withdrawn.

	Item	Pass	Fail
1	Iraqi insurgents are still capable of launching daily attacks		
2	Women have not gained most rights enjoyed by men		
3	Iraq's infrastructure such as Water, Electricity and Sanitation are still unreliable		
4	Iraq is still not pumping 90% of its oil.		

5	Iraq has not developed diplomatic relations with most nations of the world
6	Baghdad's international airport is still not open to all commercial flights
7	Unemployment rate is still high
8	Iraq's hospital and schools are still struggling to stay open and service the needs of Iraqi people
9	Iraqi's standard of living has not increased overall
10	Saddam's Palaces still stand
11	Saddam and his thugs have not been brought to trial.

Again, many more can be added to this list but for the purposes of this book, we will stick to the 11 listed here. To be honest with ourselves Americans must get a clear picture of what defeat and victory will look like when it finally comes.

Who is winning the War on Terror?

America and the world are clearly winning the war on terror. Better yet, it should be said, "America and the world are winning major battles on the war on terror." Winning battles, however, has never ever been any indication of who ultimately wins the war. During the American civil war, the Confederate Army was winning every major engagement against the superiorly equipped and trained Union army. Nevertheless, at Gettysburg, the tide turned and the Confederates were whipped by the Union.

When we listen to oratory as to how well we are doing against the terrorist we must take each win with a modest gesture of thankfulness, but we must remember that the war isn't over and it won't be over for a very long time. A lot can happen to turn the tide.

As Americans when we hear our leaders speak in grand terms as to how well America is doing in the war, we must also ask our leaders to enumerate what they believe are the battles won by the other side. Here are just a few battles the other side is winning or has already won:

• Terrorists are still capable of attacking innocent people all over the world—very recently terrorist attacked London's underground (subway) system.

- Insurgents still mount daily attacks in Iraq.

- Insurgents have still not been completely whipped in Afghanistan.

- Spain withdrew from the coalition force in Iraq.

- Somalia has become a hotbed for Terrorist training and recruitment.

Although America is winning the war on terror, we should not be lulled into believing the terrorists have not had a few victories of their own. Just as the President talks about the great strides made in the war on terror he must also clearly enumerate the losses we have suffered. It is this kind of honesty that we must expect and demand from our leaders.

Outside the scope

Although outside the scope of this book, it is important to contend with Iran's development of nuclear weapons. As described earlier, a nuclear Iran, under its current leadership and ideological principles, cannot be allowed to attain nuclear weapons. The Iranians have made no secret of their hatred of America and the west. Therefore it is imperative for the World and the United States to take a firm stand on this issue as the consequences of allowing Iran to obtain even 1 nuclear bomb can be devastating to our national security and the economic well being of the entire planet. It is imperative for the United States to act swiftly and unyielding on this issue. The President of the United States must unambiguously warn Iran that continuing on the path of obtaining nuclear weapons would put it at risks of a major air war offensive. The United States must be prepared to destroy every single military and nuclear installation Iran possesses. America can destroy Iran's entire military infrastructure without landing a single American soldier on Iranian soil. In Kosovo, America and her allies won a resounding victory solely through air attacks. If it was done in Kosovo, it can be done Iran. I would hope that the mental giants at the Pentagon are working on such a battle plan as I write.

It should also be noted here that nowhere in the world, aside from North Korea, could a man like Osama Bin Laden hide. I have no proof to back up this claim, but where else could Osama be hiding? In North Korea, among the Korean's he would stick out like a sore thumb, in Somalia and almost all other parts of the world, someone would have given him up by now in order to claim the 25 million dollar bounty on his head. The only country that can shelter Osama Bin Laden at the level he requires (governmental) is Iran. Therefore, it is easy to conclude that Osama Bin Laden is hiding in no other place but Iran. He is also probably living a relatively comfortable life among Iran's elite. If the United States ever comes across any evidence Iran's Mullah are harboring Osama Bin Laden the United States must give Iran 3 days to give him up or lose power. As Prime Minister Tony Blair warned the Taliban of Afghanistan, "Give up Osama Bin Laden or give up your power". America must firmly demand that Iran give up Osama Bin Laden or lose its power.

If America can destroy Iran's entire major military infrastructure then opposition groups from within Iran can seize power from weakened Mullahs and perhaps form a more moderate government. Naturally, it is probable a more extreme government will form but if this happens then America must be willing to again destroy any military might that regime acquires. America can do all of this without landing one single American soldier on Iranian soil thus avoiding an invasion and occupation of Iran.

As a deterrent, the United States must place enough nuclear warheads at the Iraqi and Iranian border to quickly annihilate Iran in the event of a nuclear attack upon an America city. As has been mentioned earlier, and as we can all most likely agreed upon, given Iran Mullah's hatred of Israel, it is likely a nuclear strike upon Israel will follow an attack upon the United States. Due to such a threat and in order to avoid retaliation by Israel that will only further enrage the Muslim world; the United States must prepare a massive thermonuclear strike upon Iran of at least 50–100 hydrogen bombs. These many warheads will ensure the entire Iranian landscape will be set ablaze; thus possibly preventing any nuclear warheads from leaving Iranian soil. Iran must be made fully aware of the consequences it will face if America is attacked. Iran's President Mahmoud Ahmadinejad must be made to wholly understand that any nuclear attack upon the United States will be instantaneously assumed to have been perpetuated by Iran. Because President Ahmadinejad, his family and prominent member of Iran's Mullah will have foreknowledge of an impending attack upon the United States, it is probable they will secretly leave Iran and survive annihilation of their country. Therefore, President Ahmadinejad and prominent Mullahs must be made to understand that America will pursue them without regard to national boundaries. (Let us face it, they will not hide in countries friendly to the United States—they will probably not hide in China or Russia so America will not have to violate their borders) Iran must be made to understand that America will not wait to retaliate and consider any terrorist atomic detonation over an American city as a declaration of war by Iran and therefore, America will exact colossal retribution with its entire military ferocity and vigor.

I am not advocating that waging war against Iran be America's only alternative. If the Iranian's true intentions are to provide efficient, reliable and inexpensive power to its people America has no business interfering. However, with Iran's current ideological and political rhetoric America cannot allow Iran to have the capability to produce even one atomic bomb. If Iran's nuclear intention are for peaceful means, meaning for the production of electricity then America and Europe, in exchange for Iran's abandonment of its nuclear facilities, must share technological breakthroughs in all other forms of energy in use today such as Solar , Wind Power , Geothermal , Hydroelectric and Ethanol. In exchange for Iran's abandonment of nuclear research, the United States, Europe and Iran can work collectively to hardness aforementioned forms of energy. This type of cooperation will benefit everyone as it is probable the world will run out of petroleum within the next 3–4 decades.

Therefore, while on one hand America must negotiate with Iran and offer to share technology on alternative sources of energy, America must also be clear that we cannot and will not allow Iran to continue building nuclear facilities that can easily be used to enrich weapons grade uranium.

Iran must understand the following:

a.   Iran's entire military and nuclear facilities can and will be destroyed by the United States if Iran refuses to stop enriching weapons grade uranium.

b.   Any atomic attack upon the United States will be deemed as Iran's declaration of war and will be responded to in kind with a massive American thermonuclear attack.

c.   If Iran stops, building nuclear facilities the United States will share and encourage all others to share all current forms of alternative forms of energy.

d.   The United States will, in writing, guarantee to Iran that as long as nuclear power plants and/or nuclear research is not being conducted in Iran, the United States under no circumstances will attack.

It is inevitable China and Russia will oppose any military action against Iran. However, I am quite certain that China would have annihilated Iran a long time ago if the threat was directed towards them. China has warned Taiwan with military action if its votes to establish independence. Independence only means Taiwan would formally no longer belong to China. How would China react if Iran's was developing nuclear weapons and Iran leaders had repeatedly expressed their disdain for China's communist party and had professed annihilation of China? I am quite certain China would have wiped them off the map in the early 1990s. On this note, America, would not want China to be involved in our affairs if Manhattan wanted to declare its independence. Therefore, America should not be involved in Taiwan's affairs with China. How would Americans react if China swore to come to Manhattan's defense if it ever declared independence? The unequivocal truth here is that Taiwan is a major business partner for America's rich elite so an attack by China on Taiwan would jeopardize multi-billion dollar American investments. If Taiwan were the equivalent of Madagascar, an island off the east coast of Africa, America's rich elite would not care if aliens attacked it. But then again I am outside the scope of this book. Iran's major strength is its ability to manipulate Oil Markets. Therefore, before a massive bombing campaign ensues against Iran to destroy its nuclear capabilities, the United States must freeze the price of crude oil or ask American oil producing corporations to limit their profit to a mere 100.00 dollars per second. It will be difficult for Mobil, Exxon and Shell to accept such miniscule profits as they are used to 1000.00 dollars per second, but at least we will not be asking them risk and lay down their lives as we have been asking our troops.

4

TROOPS

Increase American troop presence in Iraq to 250,000 to train and secure the country

In 1978, at age 8, I was living with my father in the capitol of San Salvador. My father was the owner of a small house divided into 4 living units and 1 bathroom. One morning my sister had gone out to the bathroom but one of my dad's tenants, as my sister was in the stall, kicked her out. My sister returned to our small apartment in tears. My dad asked her why she was crying and my sister informed my father of what had happened. Angrily my father stormed into the bathroom and dragged the lady out. He went back to bed, but only a few minutes later the lady stormed into my father's bedroom and attacked him with a machete. To protect himself, his wife and child who were in bed with him, my father caught the machete with his bare hands. His fingers were almost severed by the blow but he was able to hang on to the machete and gave the lady a well-deserved beating. Shortly thereafter I saw my father's blood soaked hands. The bones of his fingers were visible but he displayed his wound proudly. My uncle who lived in one of the apartments convinced my dad to go to the hospital. My father went grudgingly.

After my father left for the hospital my brother and I were tasked with getting breakfast for the family. And so, he and I trotted along the partly deserted streets of San Salvador on our way to the market. As we turned a corner a wave of a thousand people headed toward us. I looked up and saw soldiers firing from rooftops down to the people below. As I think back, I can still see the soldier's shoulder ricochet from the burst of each bullet leaving the muzzle of his rifle. Nevertheless, my brother and I continued walking towards the market. It was then we saw our grandfather. When he saw us, he picked us up and rushed us back to our house. My uncle told us to lie on the ground. As I laid on the floor, I could hear the screams of people in the distance. Their screams only grew louder and as their screams grew louder, I saw my sister crying and I pressed my little

50

body closer to the cold tile floor. The sounds of screaming grew louder until it was finally roaring above us. Bullets pierced the air, but just as the screams had slowly grown into a thunderous roar, they gradually dissipated. I saw my uncle cautiously stand and begin surveying the damage. My uncle then motioned for us to stand. That afternoon, the children of the neighborhood played, "Who could find the most bullet casings."

And so, I consider myself blessed to have only experienced combat at this level of severity. It was a frightening and traumatic experience. I will always remember how the shoulder of each soldier swung back with the release of each bullet. The true horror of combat is unknown to me, except for what I have seen in movies and read about so I will be the first to admit that I should not be making military recommendations. However, we have history to teach us what military leaders of the past have done when faced with aggression.

Germany launched its 'Blitzkrieg' (Lighting War) operation into Poland on the evening of August 31, 1939. England and France declared war on Germany September 3, 1939. On September 7, 1939, Churchill, First Lord of the Admiralty, proposed the creation of twenty army divisions by March 1940 with another 35 divisions by the end of 1941. It was apparent to the leaders of England and France that a major recruitment and mobilization of the countries military strength was necessary and crucial to the survival of England and France and the people of both respective countries…

The Bush administration has proposed adding an additional 40,000 troops to the military but with current recruitment goals, lagging behind it is improbable adding these many troops will happen. As has been mentioned over and over again throughout this book the President and our leader at the Federal, State and local level must galvanize the American people into fighting the war on terror as a whole. Every person in America must be persuaded to aid in the war effort. If Americans can be convinced of the necessity to stand pat and fight until we win in Iraq America will not have any issues recruiting brave and courageous young men and women to fight as they are bountiful in our society. However, if the children of our leaders continue to find safe heavens, while the children of the middle-class and poor do all the fighting, America's leaders will not be able to convince a skeptical public to send their children to fight when Bush and 99% of our Congressional leaders won't send their offspring. If we are to win the war everyone able to fight must do so.

Add a minimum of 400,000 more troops to our military.

It is baffling that both Democrats and Republicans often complain the military is stretched too thin. Are both parties saying that a war in Afghanistan, which only commands the use of 20,000 service personnel and troops in Iraq totaling 140,000 stretched our military power too thin? Most Americans will completely understand that with military bases in 18 countries and troop commitment in about 100 more the United States has tremendous military obligations. The Bush Administration has announced troop realignment, but are Americans assured that it will relieve some pressure from our military? Is this like putting a band-aid on a severed limb? On the news, several times a month we hear stories of the divorce rate among seasoned military veterans is soaring. Pick up any newspaper and you will read an article that the re-enlistment rate for GIs is at an all time low. Further compounding the military is what is being referred to as the "Back Door Draft". The "Back Door Draft is simply the extension of military service even after a GI has completed his/her contractual obligation. In the civilian world you would never agree to continue paying your mortgage after you've made your 360th payment; nor would anyone want to be forced into extending their apartment lease simply because another tenant cannot be found. This kind of "breach of contract" would never hold up in a civilian court. But our service men and women are forced to accept these types of terms everyday or face court-martial. A court-martial can result in "Dishonorable Discharge" and/or imprisonment.

The fact remains that both Democrats and Republicans are complaining about an over-extended American military. Both sides seldom agree on any issues so when they both agree on this one Americans and the folks at the Pentagon should be worried. What if China, Iran or North Korea became hostile? What is a major national emergency occurred in the United States—such as the Tsunamis of late December 2004 in the Indian Ocean where to occur here? How would America handle such emergencies if our military is already stretched too thin? Will America depend on NATO to fight the Chinese or North Korean or Iran? Americans must be prepared for a future in which 2 or three major wars have to be waged solely by the United States. Perhaps American will never have to fight 3 wars but as Americans we must be prepared to fight and defend wherever and whenever necessary. Increasing the size of the American military by 400,000 thousand should not be difficult if Americans are made aware of the real dangers posed by military stretched too thin when only 160,000 troops are fighting two separate wars.

Resurrect the Draft

During World War I and World War II and Vietnam America resurrected the draft. Now, America has always encountered problems with the draft but towards the end of the Vietnam War America had almost gotten it right. What this means is that by the early 1970s a draftee could no longer get deferment by attending college. Young, mostly rich white kids were avoiding the draft simply by attending college while poor Black, Hispanic and White kids could not dodge the draft in this fashion. Hence, the lottery emerged as a method of applying the draft across the population of young and able men. It is true that some were able to circumvent going to Vietnam by joining the National Guard, but as we know the National Guard is heavily involved in Iraq and Afghanistan, so the Army National Guard will not be a safe haven for any rich kid trying to avoid going to war. The point here is that perhaps it is time for Congress and America to start thinking of re-instating the draft. Although it will prove very unpopular, a galvanized nation, aware of a clear and present danger, will not hesitate to go along with strong leadership. A draft will also further force all the people of the United States, middle class, rich, poor, white, Hispanic, Asians, Muslims, etc, etc, to share in the dangers of war. It will not be mostly middle class and poor Americans doing most of the fighting and dying. If a draft is to be re-instated then Congress and the President must put forth a plan that will distribute the burden of war on all Americans-including old men like me.

400,000 More Troops Continued...

Throughout the Cold War America maintained superior strength as a deterrent to war and it worked. A military stretched too thin when only 2 wars are being fought will only invite countries like Iran, North Korea or China to be more aggressive. The fact remains that if America is to maintain its strength the military must be increased by at least 400,000 more troops. This number may be arbitrary as it's based solely on what others have indicated. However, assuming the number hasn't been pulled from the sky by our so called experts, to get an exact figure America must conduct a concise study of how large our military should be. Five, Seven or Ten million troops may be over kill while and addition of 400,000 may be a drop in the bucket. Only the Pentagon can make a "No Bullshit" assessment as to how many troops it will take to continue fighting in Iraq and Afghanistan, meet our military obligations and prevent our military from being stretched too thin and fight another major enemy if the need arises.

Although the question that remains is, "How many more troops do we need?" what is unquestionable is that America's military is stretched too thin.

Interesting Facts

Iraq has over 177,000 square miles. That is less than 1 American soldier to patrol each mile.

Two Hundred fifty thousand more troops need to be added in Iraq

One hundred forty thousand American servicemen and women are serving in Iraq. Some of those troops have been there past their tour of duty and some have returned after already serving 1 year. Aside from military personnel, Pentagon officials, Congress and the President, none of us really know how the war is being fought. This is not a bad thing as private citizens should not be aware of troop movements or American Military strategy. For almost 3 1/2 years, Americans have watched the war in Iraq unfold. Most of us have watched the news from the opening days of "The shock and awe" campaign to the days of car-bombings and occasional news of significant troop movement. However, aside from news of combat troop movement at the Syrian border, and several battles to oust insurgents from strongholds it seems as if American forces are in a defense position most of the time. One does not need to be a military strategist to understand that this is not how to fight guerilla type of warfare.

I am confident most Muslims (99.999%) are peace loving, good natured people who love their children. Just as most Christians, (99.999%) of them are not Ku Klux Klan members, it is safe to assume most Muslim are not terrorist…Perhaps herein lies America's biggest obstacle when fighting and engaging terrorist groups; even if their is at 100,000 its is still small compared to the estimated 2 billion Muslims throughout the world. In guerilla warfare, if your enemy is bigger than you then you become small as to attack and evade quickly with minimal capture. Hence, as the bigger and stronger power it seems to me you have two options: 1. You become even smaller than your enemy, thus becoming less of a target or 2. You amass a large army and capable of covering so much terrain that your enemy will not be able to hide or mobilize.

You Become Even Smaller Than the Enemy

Unfortunately for the United States as it become smaller, it must maintain its large army. However, in insurgency warfare, in order to rout the enemy you must not engage your troops but rather you must find tears in the enemy's defense. If your enemy uses a different language and customs than you then you must exploit dissidents within the group. If your enemy has enemies, you must get your enemies to fight each other and when they are done you fight the winner. In some ways America must allow a civil war to ensue within Iraq without favoring one group over the other until a clear winner emerges and then engage the winner in battle. (The French did not jump into the American Revolutionary War until they knew the colonials had a decent chance of winning against the British).

As I watch the evening news, I am flabbergasted by American troops patrolling Iraqi cities. Although our troops look menacing with their weapons and American insignia on practically every piece of equipment, they might as well be wearing bull's-eye. If I were a General invading a foreign country I would never parade my troops throughout the country in fancy military garb and hardware as it would only breed resentment. I do not think there is a single American who would not look at foreign troops parading or patrolling our soil with, at minimum, disdain and at worst shear hate. The bottom line is that interaction between American troops and non military Iraqis should be extremely limited. The Iraqis should not correlate insurgent activity with American presence.

America must entice its enemies to fight each other, because if they are not fighting each other there is a strong possibility they will unite; **if** that happens then America will have failed to isolate her enemies. It is therefore imperative for America to keep her enemies fighting each other as eventually they will have spent their ability to wage effective war against her. The United States must therefore encourage the enemies of the insurgents to seek and destroy them without any American intervention; except for some covert stuff here and there. Just as on American streets gang members and drug dealers mostly kill each other; if let to their own devices insurgents will start killing each other as well and all America has to do is stand back and pick up the pieces. By becoming smaller than her enemy America must also discard traditional military garb and wear into battle what her enemy wears, but because your average American will stick out like a sore thumb then America must employ Iraqis to do most of the fighting and infiltration. Paying Iraqis to work as commandos can work wonders for American in terms of defeating the insurgents.

As I drive down the interstate, I am not speeding because I am afraid there may be a State Trooper around the next bend. Most of the time there isn't but I refrain from speeding because I am afraid of that 200.00-dollar ticket and points on my license. Sometimes, I'll even slow down to below the posted speed limit as I pass a police car sitting at the side of the road only to find there is no one sitting in the vehicle. Not knowing when or where a State Trooper will be hiding deters me from speeding. Therefore, it seems obvious to me that fighting insurgents in Iraq should be done in the same fashion plain-clothes police officers fight crime. On South Florida's I-95 speeding above 100 miles per hour has become so prevalent and so rampant that police officers now patrol I-95 in undercover vehicles. On several occasions I have seen cars pulled over by Mustangs, Corvettes and Firebirds—kind of cool. The point here is that America must change its strategy on how it fights in Iraq. Conventional methods cannot work as America is not fighting a conventional army. A simple way to eliminate some road-side bomb attacks is to have all vehicles in Iraq fitted with tinted windows. "How will this help?" you ask. For one those detonating the bomb will not know who they are targeting if they cannot tell who is in the vehicle. I realize this is kind of extreme and probably impractical but the point here is that America must be creative in how it fights insurgents.

During the opening days of the Iraq war reporters told of an Iraqi convoy headed towards Baghdad. I immediately thought, "What a stupid thing for Iraqi Generals to do." It is probable that by the time the reporter had filed his story that entire convoy had been incinerated. The point here is that Iraqi insurgents, as well as most of our other enemies could never fight and defeat America using conventional warfare tactics. Therefore, their only alternative is to fight us as the insurgents in Iraq are doing now. We must then fight them as we fight crime in America. Just as they have formulated a unique strategy to fight us: suicide and car-bombings, we must device a unique strategy to fight them. Let's face it, their strategy has been so successful that in Afghanistan, America has started witnessing the same warfare tactics.

You Amass an Army so large and capable of covering so much terrain that your enemy will not be able to hide or mobilize

I have often heard that Genghis Khan would completely encircle his enemies and begin a march forward. Genghis Khan conquered much more land than Hitler and Napoleon combined and he did it all with an Army 1/10 the size of Hitler's Army. Once Khan had encircled his enemy he would order his soldiers to begin marching forward. In their wake, Khan's warriors deployed what would be a successful tactic used by the Russians during invasions by Hitler and Napoleon. The policy is called 'scorched-earth' and it's the act by which retreating troops devastate all lands and villages in the path of advancing troops as to leave nothing salvageable to the enemy. And so Khan's Army moved forward devastating and squeezing the enemy the way a snake squeezes its pray. The killing and total annihilation of everything in their wake would go on for days, weeks and even months; until Khan's Army reached the middle of the circle and complete victory was declared.

In order for America to wipe out the insurgency, the United States must amass an Army capable of forming such a circle. America can use the circle to initiate its own 'scorched-earth' policy or it can use it for the reconstruction of Iraq. I believe America would never initiate the ladder as such a policy is horrendous and it goes against our moral and ethical convictions. Such a policy would be completely and utterly "Un-American". Therefore, America has only one other option. American forces would move out from the circle instead of moving in…Everything within that circle must be reconstructed and built to conform to both Iraqi and American standards. In other words the "Green Zone" must be the starting point of that circle and from there American forces can expand outward. Obviously American forces cannot do this with 140,000 troops. Rather an endeavor of this magnitude requires at minimum 500,000 troops as it is harder to build than to destroy.

If American and Iraqis begin to build an Iraq with unsurpassed beauty and splendor the insurgents will do everything in their power to derail the progress by destroying new buildings, kidnappings, beheadings, etc, etc However, each brick laid will be a defeat to insurgents. With tight security, insurgents fighting each other and job creation through rebuilding, the insurgency will quickly die out. The creation of this circle will force America to give up some control of certain areas of the country. But as Iraqis hear of the prosperity being found in Baghdad the insurgents will have no choice but to either keep Iraqi citizen within besieged cities, thereby revealing their locations, or allow their citizens to leave and lose the protection afforded to them by being able to easily use the Iraqi populace as human shields. Furthermore, as more and more Iraqi troops are trained they will be able to provide more security to this ever-increasing circle—a circle of prosperity, life and freedom. Hence, American soldiers will be able to begin coming home.

My mother along with millions, upon millions other immigrants came to the United States because the United States was and still is a beacon of hope. As stories poured in about the quality of life in America people began to listen. What gave credence to the stories told was not American propaganda but rather the stories told came from trustworthy people; family members who had returned from America.

In March of 2005, I returned to El Salvador. My aunts and nephews were overjoyed to see me and I was delighted to be in their presence. I could tell in their eyes that they were a bit envious of me, as I had come from the United States. Nevertheless, knowing that I am not accustomed to their Llving conditions they made me feel as comfortable as possible. I was afforded the mosquito net in order to keep the mosquitoes from biting as I slept and a fan to keep me cool through the night. Even with these "conveniences", I was still unable to sleep as I got bitten by mosquitoes and became uncomfortably warm during the night. The next day my cousins and I traveled throughout El Salvador. I was happy to be in the place where I was born, but if given the choice to live there or in America I would choose America without a second thought. As I looked at my 21-year-old male cousin, Jose, I wanted to bring him to the United States so he could have the opportunity for a better life and a good career. I wanted to bring my 8-year-old cousin, Eunisis, (She is also called E.U-pronounced eh ooh—which is also the abbreviation for "Estados Unidos". In Latin America—Estados Unidos means United States) because I wanted her to grow up in a country that would provide her good nutrition, decent schools and almost endless opportunities. I wanted to bring my 17-year-old cousin, Anita, because unfortunately, in El Salvador and probably like most girls throughout third world countries, 17-year-old girls become prime candidates for marriage. Unfortunately, these marriages seldom last more than a few years and all that comes out of the marriage is several children and the woman is compelled to take care of the children on her own. So, I looked to each of my cousins and thought of ways I could help them. I knew, Anita, needed my help the most. I offered Jose financial assistance so he could start his own auto-mechanic shop and I promised my 8 year old cousin that someday I would help her come to the United States. Finally, to Anita I offered to help her come to the United States. I told her that on her 18th birthday we would begin the process of bringing her to America as a student. I offered to pay her way through a technical school where she could learn to be a Nurse's Aid or acquire any other type of certificate she can leverage in El Salvador. I told her that for 2 years I would take care of her but that after that she would need to return to El Salvador. I then said, "Who knows maybe you'll find a nice guy and you'll get married and get to stay in the United States." She looked up and smiled. What I saw in all my cousins after each conversation was a sense of hope and an ability to dream. I am telling you this story because this is exactly what I foresee happening in Iraq once the Green Zone is expanded and prosperity flourishes. With the prospects of work will come hope and 'hope' is the key ingredient to stopping suicide bombers—a major tactic used by insurgents.

When Anita turned 18 in August, as I had promised, I called and said, "Well, I am ready to begin the process of brining you to America." She was quiet for a moment and said, "Well, I've been thinking and I really don't want to go there I want to stay here and go to school." And so I said, "Oh, ok, well, then if that's what you really want then I will pay for you to attend school in El Salvador." Anita has recently started school. He vocation of choice is Airline Attendant. In El Salvador, being a flight attendant holds great prestige. Since she began school, everyone in my family has commented on her new vitality. They say, "She is so full of life and happiness now." And I think, "of course she is, she knows she has a future—she's got hope for a better life."

The simple truth is that no one wants to commit suicide if there is hope in his or her life. No one wants to die if they can see a bright future ahead. Giving the young people of Iraq the chance to a bright future is one of the keys to defeating the insurgency and defeating the urgency is the key to rebuilding Iraq and consequently winning the war!

Spoils

Some people will argue that rebuilding Iraq and providing for its security would cost too much and force us to spend too many years in Iraq. Well, this is the price America must pay for invading another country. The Iraqis did not ask for America to oust Saddam Hussein. The Iraqi people did not go to the United Nations and request the United States remove Saddam from power. The minute the United States, by force of arms, entered Baghdad their problems became ours. We are therefore, morally and ethically obligated to solve those problems. The President and Congress, by voting to invade Iraq, made the American people responsible for Iraq and we must now live and make the best of the decision we have made.

5

INFILTRATION

Stop the infiltration of insurgents into Iraq from Saudi Arabia, Syria and Iran.

Both the U.S. Military and analysis on insurgent casualties in Iraq conclude that most insurgents come from Saudi Arabia. Why is it that most insurgents killed in Iraq and most of the demonic cowards who highjacked planes on 9/11 come from Saudi Arabia? For many decades, the Saudi government taught only Islam to its male youth. Could years of brainwashing by the Saudi government now be haunting them and the rest of the world? It may be ironic that using religion to oppress the Saudi populace may come back and be the demise of the Saudi royalty. To be fair, however, the insurgents come from other parts of the world—as we saw in Afghanistan, some are even Americans. By far, however most come from Saudi Arabia, Syria and Iran—three of Iraq's neighbors.

So how can the United States prevent infiltration by would be insurgents through Iraq's borders?

American sponsored rewards leading to the capture of insurgents

In February 1979, after my mother decided she would bring my siblings and me to the United States we said our good-byes to some people we would never see again and others we would not see until we were adults. We boarded and old bus and began our journey to America. From San Salvador, we traveled through Guatemala, and continued north through Mexico. My mother was carrying 5000 dollars in cash. At bus stops, which were very numerous, policemen boarded the bus and demanded all to get off. At each stop, my mother bribed policemen and we continued our journey to the United States. In 1979, 5000 dollars was probably the equivalent of 15 or even 20 thousand dollars today but that's relative because to a person accustomed to making 50–100 dollars per week, 5000 dollars must have felt like a million! Nevertheless, my mother bribed her way to Tijuana where with the help of some friends we crossed into the United States. Once we were safely across everyone celebrated in joyous thunder. I awoke from the jeers and cheers and looked about me. I remember thinking, "This doesn't look any different than El Salvador", and went back to sleep. When I awoke the next morning and saw where we lived, I knew for sure that it was temporary and that we would soon see the evenly paved streets, beautiful homes and large playgrounds I had imagined. We lived in the ghettos of Yonkers, N.Y. until 1994 when a fire forced us to move out and into a more affluent neighborhood—a neighborhood of mostly working class Americans but still more affluent than from where we had come. The point of this story is that for the most part at the Saudi, Iranian and Syrian border the guards are probably bribed each and every day by would be insurgents. Therefore in order for America to stem the influx of insurgents into Iraq America must fight fire with fire and reward Saudi, Iranian and Syrian border guards with large sums of money leading to the capture of suspected would be insurgents. Because we do not want to be providing money to a probable enemy America must award/offer Iraqi border guards with other material goods for the exchange of information—simply providing them with large sums of cash should not be done as it will eventually not be enough to entice hungry or thirsty border guards—if you catch my drift.

Install landmines through routes traveled by insurgents

I hate to advocate landmines because of the horrendous casualties they have caused throughout Afghanistan, Vietnam and some parts of Africa decades after hostilities have ceased. Furthermore, I do not want to advocate landmines because they are against Geneva and United Nations conventions—even though these conventions did not stop the United States from attacking Iraq in the first place. Nevertheless, this is a war and we must deploy all means necessary to stop the enemy. Burying bombs along known infiltration routes within Iraqi borders and putting up signs (In several languages) of landmines will force insurgents to seek alternate routes. (Routes that can be more easily patrolled by American soldiers.) Careful mapping of these landmines can be recorded using Global Positioning devices as to allow for their removal/destruction when the war is over. Furthermore, a "smart land mine" can warn its would be victim that the bomb is ready to explode—allowing the person to move and relish in the life they have been re-given by an "American Satanist" made bomb-an opportunity terrorist do not afford their victims. These bombs can also be set to only detonate above a certain weight thereby saving the life of children and small animals. The bombs can be programmed to defuse after several years of inactivity—expiration date—if you will. I am not sure what these bombs can be made capable of, but I am sure if we can make smart bombs, we can make smart landmines.

Conduct search and destroy mission

Once landmines have been deployed and insurgents know of their location, they will seek other routes into Iraq. American forces can more easily patrol these new routes via air and land. The Chinese built the Great Wall of China to keep invaders at bay. America must deploy small elite forces throughout Iraq's border to keep insurgents at bay. America must warn the risk of bodily injury to all those entering militarized border zones. Ambush type tactics must be implemented. The insurgents by nature are not the sharpest minded people on earth and therefore some will walk across that mine field and die while others even after having been warned against entering a militarized zone will enter and be shot to death. While some insurgents will be lucky and make it to Baghdad, with American quadrupled reconstruction efforts, they will find a growing and prosperous capitol—perhaps they then too will search for work as carpenters, welders, and bricklayers instead of insurgents or suicide bombers. Before long, just as Mexicans & Central Americans cross into the United States looking for work, Iraq will see an influx of young men and women eager to take jobs not wanted by Iraqis; such a janitors, motel employees, bus boys, crop pickers, house cleaners; just like in America. I can see it now, an Iraqi Lou Dobbs, running stories about how "immigrants" are ruining Iraq.

Relocate all villages and towns along borders or pay village elders for information leading to the capture of suspected insurgents

America has two choices. We can either relocate what I assume to be hundreds, maybe even thousands of small villages through Iraq's border or we can simply offer money or material goods leading to the capture of insurgents. Personally, I do not think people should be relocated because it causes too much confusion and often the places where people are relocated to resemble concentration camps or prisons. This is a big no, no! Therefore, America has only one choice—entice village people to give away suspected insurgents. Some may argue that it would cost too much to entice people to give away insurgents. What I am saying is that if Manhattan Island can be bought from the Indians for a few European goods, then America can buy Iraqi village elders with a few commodities easily accessible to us but extremely difficult for them to attain.

American Troops should patrol Iraqi Borders

Iraqi's should not patrol Iraq's borders. Unfortunately, most Iraq's troops cannot be trusted simply because the country is still in turmoil and experiencing extreme poverty. Iraqi border patrol agents/troops cannot be trusted to resist the temptation of accepting bribes from would be insurgents. Winning the war in Iraq is heavily dependent on defeating insurgents. And the defeat of the insurgency does not lie with the capture of "suspected" insurgents in the capitol. Massive sweep and arrest of "suspected" insurgents only create resentment and animosity as some if not most "suspected" insurgents captured are probably innocent. After 9/11, the FBI arrested thousands of people and to date only one person has been charged in relation to the 9/11 attacks. Although no one has reported on the resentment, this massive incarceration of people spawn it is quite clear that most people would be resentful towards the government if imprisoned unjustly. Therefore, the key to defeating the insurgency lies at the Iraqi borders.

Today, August 10, 2005, I heard Donald Rumsfeld, demanded to know from the Iranians how some Iranian military equipment got into Iraq. I then heard the news commentator say, "It is obvious the Iranians are not doing a good job of preventing arms shipment and insurgents from crossing into Iraq." I immediately thought, 'Are you telling me that you expect the Iranians to do a job in the best interest of America'. That's like asking drug lords to patrol the waters off south Florida from drug trafficking or asking Fidel Castro to live up to the true ideals of communism and live in as much poverty as his people do. (But that too is another book). Americans should be the only ones completely in charge of patrolling all of Iraq's borders as Americans are the only ones who benefit from stopping the infiltration of arms shipments and fresh jihad recruits into Iraq.

6

IRAQI SECURITY FORCES

Strengthen and train the Iraqi Police and military forces.

Americans should rejoice in the fact that the U.S government has launched massive recruiting efforts to draw volunteer Iraqi police and military personnel. Some Iraqi personnel are already conducting mission with American soldiers. Recently American and Iraqi troops launched operation Lightning in which 1500 suspected insurgents were captured. This is a good start. However, a division of 18,000 men is not expected to be fully operational until October 2005 or in early 2006. The number of Iraqi Para-military/military personnel appears fluid as America was told by the President that 100,000 troops have been trained while the U.S. Commander, Maj. Gen. William G. Webster Jr. said he will have 18,000 troops ready to secure Baghdad by October 2005. Who are Americans to believe? Nevertheless, it is unknown to me why it would take 2 years to train someone to essentially serve as a "security guard" In the United States police officers generally required 12 weeks of training. In Iraq, even under the best of circumstances, the United States does not have the luxury to spend 3 months training an Iraqi to serve and protect. The United States should not be training Iraqis in the fashion an American soldier or police officer is trained. The security situation in Baghdad and throughout all of Iraq does not permit it. Certainly, it would be feasible to have superior training but at the present time, Iraq cannot afford it. Therefore, enough training should be provided to ensure a reasonable amount of success. Any person with some law enforcement experience will tell you that often, the mere presence of uniformed security officers is enough to deter crime. Therefore, if the United States can put 200,000 security forces in place throughout Iraq then perhaps their presence will be enough to deter insurgent attacks.

No formidable Iraqi Army

The United States has in the past helped some countries build a strong military through arms sales. In the 1980s, the United States sold weapons to the Saddam Hussein's regime. In the 1990, Saddam used some of those weapons to attack Kuwait. The point here is that the United States should not allow Iraq to maintain a formidable army as America may be forced to fight it later. Of course, Iraq should be allowed to maintain an army for the protection of its sovereignty, but America should not be training and/or arming Iraq to the tee.

Nay Sayers

Assuming America empowers the Iraqis to build an Army and secure itself then what assurances, do Americans have Iraq will not turn that Army against the United States? What if Iran and Iraq form an alliance and decide to defy the will of the United States? Will America then go to war against the Army it helped build? As unlikely as these scenarios sounds nothing can be ruled out of the realm of possibilities. It would be very embarrassing for the United States to have to fight Iraq in 7–10 years. Therefore, victory in Iraq cannot be declared from simply arming Iraq. Victory can only be declared after Iraq has achieved a modest level of prosperity for all its varied ethnics groups.

NATO

Once Iraq has been reconstructed and most of the objectives outlined earlier in this book have been achieved then perhaps Iraq can begin the process of joining the North Atlantic Treaty Organization. Ukraine, once part of the Soviet Alliance, has recently declared its bid to join NATO. By joining NATO Ukraine will be part of alliance that would help it in the event of an attack by a hostile nation. If Iran emerges as a Nuclear power over the next few years, it will be imperative for Iraq to be part of the NATO Alliance as it would assure that a conventional or nuclear attack upon Iraq would be responded to in kind. Iraq would also be a great ally if NATO has to forcefully disarm Iran.

If policing are the only jobs that exist make sure those jobs pay well

The Average pay for an Iraqi soldier is approximately 60 dollars per month. While the average pay for a policeman is approximately 120 dollars per month. If anyone faces more danger in Iraq than American soldiers it is the Iraqi security forces. In Iraq 60 or 120 dollars per month may be substantial, but even at 100,000 dollars per year how many Americans would choose to be police officers in a country, the size of Texas, where on average 5–10 officers die per day? It is probable not many Americans would heed the call.

Even with such odds, Iraqi young men and women flock to recruiting stations and volunteer. Do they do it for love of their country or for the monetary reward? We should probably think its for both. Because the dangers are so great, America must increase the pay to 500–1000 dollars per month. In Iraq that kind of money may be equivalent to an American making 5000–10,000 dollars per month, I am not sure; nevertheless, it is a lot of money. This kind of money may even entice some insurgents to lay down their arms and volunteer for Iraqi security forces. Furthermore, a well-paid Iraqi security force will have financial means to propel the Iraqi economy. Naturally this will add to the daily price tag of fighting the war in Iraq, but we must remember that Iraqis did not invite Americans unto their land therefore we are morally and ethically responsible for the country's well being.

In the United States, after the 9/11 attacks, the President extended the benefits of all unemployed persons. His basic argument for the extension was that if Americans had money to spend they would propel the economy. The same logic flows for increasing the average pay of an Iraqi security officer.

Furthermore a dramatic increase in salary for Iraqi personnel will enable America and Iraqi authorities to demand more from their recruits and although monetary compensation doesn't always retain your employees it goes a long way to keeping someone around. In my case, I stuck around with the same stinky company, installing and supporting an awful CTI software application because the money was good.

7

RECONSTRUCTION

Quadruple reconstruction Efforts

There isn't a single more important aspect of wining the war in Iraq than the rebuilding of the country. After years of Saddam's rule and several devastating wars, Iraq is in ruins. Most Americans have never traveled to Iraq and neither have I, but on our nightly news we have all seen areas of devastation and extreme poverty. America cannot expect to build a few schools and hospitals and consider reconstruction to be completed. The people of Iraq must see a significance change in their quality of life, government and country in order to feel that the hardships, deaths and misery suffered throughout American occupation were not in vain.

I move to Florida on July 27, 1998. When I arrived in Florida, there were still empty lots and wooded areas near I-75 in Pembroke Pines in the county of Broward. Broward is just north of Miami-Dade County. Route 27 runs at the northeast end of the Everglades. Many years ago, Florida State government built a prison in that area. Now, because there is such few land available, developers want to build on land next to the prison, but they are afraid that with the prison being so close by people will refuse to buy. So, some developers have petitioned the government to move the prison. I laugh at this because it is usually the other way around. The government usually ends up fighting the local communities when a prison or an infrastructure with a certain level of stigma is proposed.

I am telling this story because I am amazed at the amount of growth I have seen in South Florida in only 7 years. Its almost as if the buildings have gone up over night. This explosive growth has created jobs and lifted the wealth of South Floridians. (South Florida has one of the lowest unemployment rates in the country) The land where my house sits only 3 years ago was a farm. Now there are over 800 beautiful homes where sugar canes once grew.

Therefore, the rebuilding of Iraqi's infrastructure will surely create jobs and propel the Iraqi economy forward. As Americans, we must understand that for at least the next few years we will need to bear the burden of rebuilding that country. Perhaps next time America will be more cautious when invading another country.

The current construction efforts in Iraq are good but they are not good enough or near where they should be. By the time you read this book, if before the end of 2006, America will be have occupied Iraq for over 3 1/2 years. Yet, Iraqis do not have reliable electricity, water facilities and many other infrastructures necessary to propel a country's economy and the well being of its people. After 3 1/2 years Iraq is still not producing the amount of oil required to sustain its economy. At the outset of the war, the President proclaimed that getting Iraq to begin pumping oil was crucial for Iraq to pay for all the needed materials to rebuild. It was obvious to me that it was a good idea because Iraqi oil would help the American and World economy while helping the Iraqis. "At last," I thought, "The Iraqi people will benefit from the country's wealth." from the country's wealth. Every Iraqi citizen is entitled to enjoy the wealth, which lies beneath his or her feet. Nevertheless, the oil is not pumping to the capacity expected even after 2 1/2 years of American occupation.

In September of 2004, Hurricane Frances struck South Florida's Palm Beach County. (Please note President Bush was in Palm Beach handing out water the day after hurricane Frances hit. It took him 4 days to get to New Orleans after Katrina) Out of curiosity, as the storm swirled through most of the county, I stepped outside my home and watched the wind bend the palm trees with ferocity I had never witnessed. Every few seconds the sky lit up a strange blue. I thought it was weird that lighting would be a blue color. After a few minutes of standing outside, common sense entered my head and I ran back inside the house. When I entered the house I explained to my wife the ominous blue lights in the sky and she said, "Oh, That's transformers exploding" I thought, "That explains the blue color." Throughout the night, the lights inside our home had flickered on and off until at 1:30 a.m. the lights finally went out for good. It would be 3 days before electricity came on again. I can almost assure you that if the people of West Palm Beach had to wait 2 1/2 weeks to get reliable electricity; most elected officials running for re-election would have lost their re-elections bid in November. The Iraqi people have had to endure 3 1/2 years of unreliable electrical service—service interrupted by the "Shock and Awe" campaign. Most Americans completely understand that the Iraqis were copping with power outages before our invasion but as said earlier, the moment American troops crossed the border into Iraq—their problems became ours and the grievances they had been unable to air to their own government would be clearly enumerated to an American government.

The point being made here is that if Iraqis cannot count on reliable electricity and water how can Americans think other constructions efforts are moving along rapidly when reliable electricity and water are key components of any rebuilding project and definitely key components to a comfortable life as we Americans know it.

As an unemployed person, I recently searched for work in Iraq. There were a total of about 50 job openings in Iraq for Americans. About 50% of the jobs, where for Intelligence gathering personnel while 35%s were for construction project managers, the rest were for field technicians and wireless communications analyst. Iraq is in desperate need of repair to almost every component necessary to build a prosperous country. Therefore, 50 job openings are pathetic. The skeptic must be thinking, "Well, that's because most of the jobs are occupied by Iraqis." If that's true then how do we explain 23% unemployment in Iraq?

Interesting Fact

If the United States experienced 23% unemployment, we would be looking at over 30 million unemployed men and women. 30 Million Unemployed people would cause dramatic poverty and misery in the United States. Who would America blame for such misery and poverty; the invaders or those fighting the invaders? It must be conceded, however, that Iraq had high unemployment rate before America's occupation, but the minute American troops crossed into Iraq—their problems became ours.

These numbers therefore lead me to believe that the reconstruction is slow at best. The reconstruction of Iraq must be quadrupled and Iraqis must see the fruit of their labor flourish.

I cannot pretend to know what it takes to rebuild Iraq, but I do know the rebuilding of Iraq is crucial to America's success. Our leaders in Washington need to formulate and execute a comprehensive plan for rebuilding Iraq in 2–5 years. As the rebuilding starts and the country flourishes, it is probable that the insurgency will subside—because jobs will be created. Once the insurgency subsides and Iraqis are securing the country Americans can begin withdrawing from and inserting a mostly Muslim division of American troops. Troops. When I traveled to El Salvador in March of 2005, I was amazed at the explosive growth. In some areas I felt as if I was still in America. Although poverty and crime is still quite high, talk of armed revolution is non-existent. Rebuilding has created jobs and jobs have created hope. Furthermore, the influx of El Salvadorans entering the

United States has diminished. During the 10 years of Civil War in El Salvador over 500,000 El Salvadoran migrated to the United States. I am not sure what the numbers are today, but I am willing to bet Lou Dobbs it isn't nearly what it was in the mid 80s.

My Father-in-Law, Suicide Bombers and me

My father-in-law was laid-off from GM over 4 years ago. For the first few, months and up to a year he steadfastly looked for work but after years of no success, he gave up. My father in law is 64 years old. He often jokes that it would be good for him to die before he turns 70. "If I die before 70" he jokes, Alice (my mother-in-law) "gets 100,000 dollars in life insurance. After 70 she doesn't get anything." My wife and mother-in-law only look at each other in dismay and fright. I must also admit that several times after being let go from my job I thought that perhaps committing suicide would be a good alternative. My wife would get 350,000 dollars in life insurance, my entire 401k and some social security benefits. Every time I had those thoughts, I shook my head and thought, "What am I thinking; that's totally crazy." and I go about searching for work via the Internet.

The point I am trying to make here is that if my father-in-law and I can think of our deaths as beneficial (I am confident I was not the first unemployed person to have such thoughts) to our families how can we as Americans not think that a suicide bomber in Iraq, who has been promised riches in heaven, virgins galore and a stipend to his family, not view suicide as the only viable alternative to him/her? From a suicide bombers perspective, after suffering the humiliation of an invasion and occupation, 23% unemployment, complete degradation of living conditions and loss of all hope, will, of course, of course think suicide bombings isn't such a bad alternative; furthermore, with all the hate he or she has been taught since he/she was but a little boy or a girl it doesn't take a rocket scientist or PH.D in psychology to come to the conclusion that the suicide bomber will not only be eager to complete his mission but will relish it and attempt to inflict as much damage as possible. And to think Iraq may have hundreds upon thousands of these young men and women simply waiting in the wings. How can America overcome such mentally by would be suicide bombers? The simple answer is to create JOBS—jobs will create hope and hope of a better life will make suicide bombers think twice. Rebuilding of Iraq's entire infrastructure will create jobs and therefore the rebuilding of Iraq should be paramount on our agenda; even higher than training Iraqi troops to secure the country.

I recently started working again and the though of committing suicide has not entered my mind at all...thank goodness...I thought I was going crazy!

CONCLUSION

Americans must understand that victory in Iraq does not mean we will return to pre 9/11 days. As Americans we must be proud of the military and economic might our labor has brought us. Nations and organizations willing to challenge the United States have two choices: engage America on a battlefield and go into the fight certain of defeat or brainwash a group of young men to use the freedoms we cherish to infiltrate our society and attack innocent unarmed civilians within our own borders. Knowing they cannot defeat us on a battlefield, they will attack our cities and kill our innocent men, women and children.

The United States must hardness its economic might to help rebuild Iraq. After the attacks of 9/11, the cleanup of the World Trade Center took about 6 months; much less than had been anticipated. New York City and its neighboring counties banded together and formed a tremendous effort to collectively remove the debris left over from the collapse of the Twin towers. Why was it so crucial to remove the debris? It was crucial for the continuity of business as usual in New York and for the people of the United States and specially New Yorkers to move forward. What kind of an affect would lingering debris from such an awful hate act have on the psyche of New Yorkers and Americans? As Iraqi's look around them and see destroyed buildings and foreign troops on their land they must feel a sense of shame and embarrassment? How would Americans feel about foreign troops on our land? What if debris from the collapsed Twin Towers still littered the streets of lower Manhattan? It is imperative for America to train Iraqi troops, rebuild the country and leave the country better off than it was under Saddam Hussein. The key here is a better Iraq than under Saddam Hussein—think, how difficult can it really be to leave behind an Iraq better than it was under Saddam Hussein?

When I was a child my mother was married to a man who was, by today's standards, a militant. In the early 1980's, El Salvador was engaged in a bloody civil war. The United States under Ronald Reagan, in order to stop the spread of communism and prevent the "Domino Theory" in Central America, was aiding the brutal and often murderous Salvadoran government with billions of dollars in arms. I was but 10 years old at the time but my mother's ex-husband would take me to political rallies at which films depicting the guerilla type war being waged

71

in El Salvador by the FMLN were shown. The rallies were often held in people's homes or in "out-of-the-way" saloons. Even though I was but a boy I was being indoctrinated into what now would be considered "Terrorist" mentality. At the time I could not wait to grow up so that I could join the fight in El Salvador and help the FMLN and the El Salvadoran people overthrow their brutal government. Often times my mother's ex-husband would tell her that I would someday grow up to be a great leader. He taught me to embrace and believe in the ideals of communism. I am sure if my mother had stayed married to this man, I would have grown up full of hate against the United States for backing a murderous El Salvadoran regime who assassinated 58,000 El Salvadorans during the 12 years of civil war (1980–1992). After my mother divorced this man in 1982, I never heard or saw him again. I had heard my mother's ex-husband had moved back to El Salvador after the divorce so in March of 2005 when I traveled to El Salvador, I asked my uncle about him. My uncle said, "Yes, he is still alive, he's an old man now." I then said to my uncle, "The next time I come to El Salvador I'd like to meet him. I want to tell him how wrong he was about Communism." My uncle only smiled. My political views have changed dramatically since I was a 10-year-old child, but I wonder what would have happened to me if I had continued being indoctrinated in such a fashion. Would hate taught from such a young and impressionable age have driven me to commit the acts 19 hijackers committed on September 11, 2001? The point here is that hate against the United States is spewed in the Middle East and America must rise above it and prove to the Muslim world that America is not a land of Satanists and Infidels. Iraq is a great place to start. If we can rebuild Iraq into a country equitable to all its varied ethnic and religious groups then perhaps Iraq will be the beacon of hope needed so very desperately throughout the Middle East. To rebuild Iraq into a prosperous and free nation will fly in the face of what has been and is being taught to their children.

Perhaps rebuilding Iraq into a prosperous free nation is the silver lining arising out of the clouds of September 11, 2001.

The End

978-0-595-38110-4
0-595-38110-3